D0291704

Acknowledgments

By providing the opportunity to benefit one another, a book contributes to, and can even constitute, friendship. This book is no exception. Looking back upon it, I am grateful to those from whom I benefited. Looking forward, I am hopeful of the possibility of the like.

Stephen Esposito persuaded me of the need and usefulness of a comparison between the two apologies. Richard Buckwalter, who has been a fellow companion from the beginning to the end, helped me to carry out the labors. Norma Thompson and Michael Palmer reviewed the manuscript and made astute corrections and suggestions. I am thankful for the generous assistance of all.

Mark Kremer

2005

Preface

Socrates was accused of impiety and of corrupting the youth. Since ancient Athenian democracy had no separation of church from state, these religious accusations were also legal charges. He was eventually tried, convicted, imprisoned, and executed though both Plato and Xenophon make clear that the charges were not brought forward in the spirit of true piety, and that Socrates was a man of real virtue and beneficence. To this day, his trial and execution remain a mark upon the democracy that put him to death.

Socrates would have certainly avoided the hemlock were he born into our modern democracy, but that is not to say that he would be free to live his life of questioning. It is not even to say that the modern state is more tolerant of philosophy than ancient democracy. Athens was not as hostile to Socrates as one might first suppose, nor are we as open to him as we like to believe. Had Socrates wished, he could have easily avoided his guilty sentence and his execution. Plato makes this clear in a number of ways and Xenophon states it outright. Furthermore, the vehemence with which Socrates is today condemned by our educational overseers surpasses Athenian democracy's hatred for him. If we would not kill him, it is only because we have invented other ways in which to silence his questions.

Socrates is today condemned for being the founder of Western rationalism. The ancient democracy condemned him for not being a believer in the gods of the city while our "postmodern" or late democracy condemns him for being a believer in "truth", which is said to be relative.

In its democratic expression, relativism assumes progress towards ever-greater democracy is good and necessary. While this belief is not considered religious, because it seems to have no god, one could, nonetheless, argue that it partakes of the religious and does have a god. While democratic relativism recognizes no revealed or traditional god, it believes in a world-historical god of progress that promises to deliver mankind from all hierarchy, restraint, and the strife accompanying them.

Democratic relativism is, then, not an insight or awareness but an idea used to further a certain understanding of democratic freedom and equality. This relativism is contradictory since it affirms the goodness of democracy, as well as its freedoms and equalities.

Democratic relativism is an attempt to avoid an account of democratic beliefs by asserting that such beliefs cannot be justified in principle, and, therefore, that one ought not even expect an account. This kind of unaccountable faith is for Socrates, really a form of obscurantism and conventionalism. The denial in principle that democratic opinion has any foundation suggests that the belief in democracy is founded on nothing more than the arbitrary agreement and authority of its adherents, who are protected from the need for argument by the popular acceptance of democracy. Democratic relativism is, therefore, a form of democratic conformity; it is *agnoew* or lacking in awareness, because it does not comprehend its own intentions and contradictions.

To the extent that humanity requires thoughtfulness about beliefs and a willingness to defend them, democratic relativism has weakened humanity instead of strengthening it. What pretends to be the greatest openness is really the greatest prejudice or complete unwillingness to listen and to defend. This intolerance masquerading as openness has the same essential character as the ancient religious beliefs of Athens with one important difference: ancient orthodoxy was not nihilistic but actually believed in a world that supported its faith, and in this way is actually more rational than the dogma of our progressives.

True openness requires that we embrace Socrates who was the gadfly to the democracy in which he lived, forcing his fellows to justify their lives and teaching them that the unexamined life is not worth living. Whether the prejudice in question was 'progressive' or 'traditional' was of no consequence to him. He brought humanizing doubts to bear upon cherished beliefs.

In addition to being ignorant of its own conventional character, democratic progressives deride past thinkers by exaggerating their dependency on their times. Plato and Xenophon were not unthinking slaves to the prejudices of their class, gender, or the Greek polis, but were self-conscious founders of new traditions, and, as such, broke with their time.

Plato's Socrates was intended to be the pattern of nature, and his example was meant to be the foundation for the Academy. The *Apology*, in particular, is the work most responsible for establishing the possibility and ideal of the university—a place where the philosopher can get his free meal and have some recognition of his claim to be a great benefactor and to be more worthy of admiration than national heroes.

It is customary to translate Plato's *Apology* with all or some of the *Euthyphro*, *Crito*, and *Phaedo*, because these dialogues, taken together, make up what are called 'the last days of Socrates'. The *Euthyphro* takes place before his trial, the *Apology* at his trial, the *Crito* at his imprisonment awaiting execution, and the *Phaedo* at his death. Although these dialogues are dramatically related, I have chosen not to translate them together, but instead to translate Plato's *Apology of Socrates* with Xenophon's. By studying them together one gains a clearer understanding of the different intentions of Plato and of Xenophon, and, therewit, a deeper understanding of both the *Apologies* and the nature of philosophy.

When I translated Plato's *Cleitophon*, I said that there was no great need for a new translation, and that my main intention was to provoke and defend thought. The same holds with respect to this work. Mine are not the first translations aspiring towards literalness, and I have benefited from many, including Reeves' book,[1] which contains translations of both *Apologies*. The Wests,[2] however, have been most helpful because they have been most literal. I differ from them, not only by including Xenophon's *Apology*, but by trying to overcome the jarring awkwardness that often accompanies literalness. I have also sought a tone that is true to the nature of the drama. An Athenian trial ought not to sound either pedantic or familiar and personal, not even when it is Socrates' trial. The *Apology* is the only public speech given by Socrates. It is, of course, less a defense of the public than a defense of himself and of the life of philosophy. The speech is, therefore, by its very nature insolent in so far as he chooses to judge the public rather than to excuse himself before it. Plato's Socrates even ridicules and humiliates his accuser Meletus in a manner that Socrates knows has and will make himself hated.

Plato is trying to capture what he thinks philosophy's relation should be to the people. When Socrates periodically raises the ire of the jury, the Wests, following Liddell and Scott, translate his admonitions as "Please do not make a disturbance." This is overly polite and more in accord with the manners of the schoolroom than either Athenian politics or Socratic speech. Jowett, whose translation aims to be familiar rather than literal, translates the admonitions as "[do] not interrupt me," which is far too personal. Socrates is inciting the anger of the crowd and they are clamoring against him. In fact, he is consciously provoking them and falls just short of calling them a mob. His admonitions are moments where we get to measure the reaction of the crowd to what he says and how he responds to them. He does not attempt to

---

1   C.D.C. Reeve, *The Trials of Socrates: Six Classic Texts* (Hackett Publishing Company, Inc., 2002).

2   Thomas G. West and Grace Starry West, *Four Texts on Socrates* (Cornell University Press, 1984).

assuage their anger but continues to provoke them, and certainly does not flatter their passions in order to win favor with them. The crowd is incensed by what appears to them as insolence and they have no articulate reaction other than noisy outrage.

Socrates, however, is far more than a provocateur. It is easy to shock and insult, but he does so in the name of philosophy. Consequently, he has been called a martyr on behalf of philosophy. Whether it is sufficient to think of him as a martyr any more than as a provocateur is doubtful. The nature of philosophy or of the free mind is somewhere between shameless agitation and high-minded martyrdom. The discovery of this meaning is the most important reason to return to the two *Apologies*.

Plato and Xenophon
APOLOGIES

PLATO and XENOPHON
APOLOGIES

**Translated, with
Interpretive Essay and Notes**

Mark Kremer

focus an imprint of
Hackett Publishing Company, Inc.
Indianapolis/Cambridge

Apologies

© 2006 Mark Kremer
Previously published by Focus Publishing/R. Pullins Company

focus an imprint of
Hackett Publishing Company, Inc.
P.O. Box 44937
Indianapolis, Indiana

www.hackettpublishing.com

All rights reserved. Printed in the United States of America

20 19 18 17   6 7 8 9 10

ISBN: 978-1-58510-188-7

CONTENTS

Plato's *Apology of Socrates*[3]

SOCRATES: In what way you, Athenian men, have been moved by   17a
my accusers, I do not know. As for myself, even I almost forgot myself
on account of them, so persuasively did they speak. And yet, in a way,
they said nothing true. I wondered, most of all, at one of the many
falsehoods which they told–the one in which they said that you need
to be on guard lest you should be deceived by me, as I am a clever
speaker. That they are not ashamed that they will be immediately   b
refuted by me in deed, when I appear in no way to be a clever speaker,
seemed to me to be most shameful of them, unless of course they call
the one who speaks the truth a clever speaker. For if this is what they
are saying, then I would agree that I am an orator, though not of their
sort. As I say, therefore, they have said little or nothing true, but from
me you will hear the whole truth. By Zeus, Athenian men, neither
speeches beautified like theirs with phrases and words, nor contrived,   c
but rather you will hear what is spoken in words as they happen at
random, since I trust the things I say to be just. And let none of you
expect otherwise. For surely, it is not fitting, men, for someone of my
age to come before you like a youth making up speeches. And above
everything, Athenian men, I beg and implore this of you. If you hear
me defend myself with the very speeches I am accustomed to speak
both in the marketplace at the counters, where many of you have
heard me, and elsewhere, neither be amazed nor clamor[4] because of   d

---

3   The word for apology is *apologia* and can be used to mean legal defense, but is used
    by both Plato and Xenophon to mean something deeper, as in the accounting or
    justification for one's very existence, which can be justified by nature as opposed
    to law or *nomos*. The defense speech to the jury is almost equivalent to defending
    oneself in assembly or before the city as a whole. There is no judge and instruction
    in law, and one can bring in personal matters such as the suffering of one's family.
    Socrates' defense speech is really a defense to the city and not just to a judge, jury,
    and law in our sense.

4   The verb to clamor is *thorubein*. It is an insult that characterizes the indignation of
    the jury as noisy and pointless. Since we do not hear the jury speak, their decision
    appears in the light of Socrates' characterization of them.

1

this. For it holds thus: for the first time, before a court of justice I come, at the age of seventy. Therefore, I am simply foreign to the ways of speaking here. If I happened to be a foreigner, you would surely sympathize with me if I spoke in the dialect and way in which I was

18a   raised, likewise I also beg it of you now, and it is just as it appears to me. Disregard my way of speaking, for perhaps it is worse, perhaps better, but rather consider this alone and apply your mind to it: whether or not the things I say are just. For this is the virtue[5] of a judge, that of an orator, to speak the truth.

First, then, I am right to defend myself, Athenian men, against the first false accusations and my first accusers, and then next against

b   the later accusations and the later accusers. To you, many have accused me from long ago and already for many years, yet they say nothing true. Of them, I am more afraid than of Anytus[6] and those among him, though they too are dangerous. But those are more dangerous, men, the one's laying hold of many of you since childhood, who persuaded you and accused me of nothing true: that there is a Socrates, a wise man, a ponderer on the things above, and one who has investigated all the things under the earth and makes the weaker speech stronger.[7]

c   Those ones, Athenian men, who have spread this report are my dangerous accusers, since the ones who listen think that those who investigate these things do not believe in the gods. Furthermore, these accusers are many and have accused me for a long time and, moreover, said these things to you in those years in which you are most trusting, some of you being children and some youths, and they accused me

---

5   The word for virtue is *aretē* and it means excellence. The excellence of a thing need not be moral. The word for truth is *alētheia*. Socrates emphasizes the intellect by distinguishing virtue and truth from passion and prejudice.

6   Anytus was a tanner, who became wealthy and eventually held a leading political position in the democracy. In Xenophon's *Apology*, Socrates suggests that Anytus' hatred was the real animus for the trial. Socrates blames Anytus for ruining his own son, who had a noble soul requiring a noble activity and object, but who was ruined by sensual passions because his father provided for him coarse and plebian duties. Socrates suggests that participation in politics is for coarse souls.

7   The accusation of being a wise man is related to both the formal charges and to Aristophanes' play the *Clouds,* where Socrates is shown studying natural science and teaching rhetoric. The study of natural science threatens the belief in the gods by giving natural explanations to heavenly movements and occurrences. By looking beneath the earth, Socrates threatens the beliefs in Hades in addition to the cosmic gods. The accusation of making the weaker speech the stronger suggests that he disrupts the divine order by assisting injustice to triumph over justice through the art of rhetoric.

in a case that was entirely by default, there being no one to defend. And, the thing most unaccountable of all is that it is impossible to know and to say their names, unless one should be a comic poet.[8] They persuaded you using envy and slander and the ones having been persuaded themselves, persuaded others. All of these are most difficult to deal with, for to bring any of them forward here is not possible, nor to refute any of them, but it is simply necessary, as if fighting shadows, to speak in my defense and to refute with no one to respond. You too consider it to be exactly as I say—that there are two groups of accusers, the ones accusing me now and the ones long ago of whom I speak. And, consider it necessary as well to first defend myself against these first, because both earlier and much more than the later ones did you hear them accusing me.

18d

e

Well then, a defense speech is necessary, O Athenian men, as well as an attempt to remove from you, in the little time here, the slander that you acquired over much time.[9] I would wish things might be like that, were it in any way better for both you and me, and that I, in making a defense speech, might accomplish something. I consider this to be hard and I am not entirely forgetful of it. Nonetheless, let it be in whatever way is dear to the god, though it is necessary to obey the law and to make a defense speech.

19a

Let us take up, therefore, from the beginning what the accusation is from which the slander against me has arisen—and in which Meletus trusted when he wrote the indictment against me. Well then, whatever did the slanderers say in their slanders? Just like accusers, their charge must be read: "Socrates does injustice and is a busybody, investigating the things beneath the earth and in the heavens and making the weaker speech the stronger, and teaching these things to others." It is like this. You yourselves have also seen such things in the comedy of Aristophanes, a Socrates paraded about claiming to walk on air and spouting much other nonsense about which I have no knowledge, neither much nor little. I do not say this in order to dishonor this kind of knowledge, if anyone is wise in such subjects, only let me not be prosecuted by Meletus on such charges, for, in fact, Athenian men, I have no share in these matters. As witnesses, I offer once more yourselves, and I deem it well that you teach and also tell one another—the ones of you who

b

c

d

---

8   Aristophanes, who parodied Socrates' wisdom in the *Clouds*.

9   A trial for a capital offense was circumscribed by a very limited amount of time, indicating little concern with the truth.

at anytime heard me conversing, and many are such ones among you, if ever, either little or great, anyone of you heard me conversing about such things, and from this you will see that it is likewise for the other things that the many say concerning me.

But, in fact, neither are these things so, and if you have heard
19e   from anyone that I attempt to educate human beings and take money, neither is that true either. Though this too seems to me to be noble,[10] if one should be able to educate human beings just as Gorgias the Leontine, and Prodicus the Ceon, and Hippias the Elean.[11] For of these, each, men, is able, going into each of the cities, to persuade the
20a   young, who can be with, for free, any of their own citizens whom they wish, to abandon being with these ones and to be with themselves and to give them money and to show thanks besides.

And there is another wise man from Parios here, who I thought was residing in town, for I chanced to encounter a Callias,[12] son of Hipponicus, who has paid out more money to sophists than all others taken together. Therefore, I questioned him, for he had two sons— "Callias," I said, "if your sons were born colts or calves, then we could get and hire for them an overseer, who would make both of them
b   noble and good in the virtue belonging to them, he being someone from either horsemen or farmers. But now, since they are human beings, who do you have in mind to get to oversee them? Who is a knower of such virtue—that of a human being and also of a citizen? For I suppose you have carefully considered it, on account of your having two sons. Is there someone," I said, "or not."

"Very much so" he said.

---

10   The word for noble is *kalon*, which also means beautiful. The use of the same word for noble and for beautiful is indicative of how the Greeks understood the relation of soul to appearance. The beauty of the outer appearance is meant to reflect the soul or the capacity for noble activity. For example, the beauty of Achilles' body contains the expectation of the soul capable of his noble deeds. Socrates reforms the Greek understanding of the noble, since he is famously ugly but claims to have true beauty of soul.

11   These men are sophists. Aristophanes taught that Socrates had an affinity to them. Socrates, however, emphasizes his differences and especially his purer soul (he does not take money), and he does not make unfounded and proud claims to knowledge. One of Plato's many poetic achievements is to sublimate the art of rhetoric and sophistry towards philosophy through the art of the dialogue.

12   Callias was a wealthy Athenian famous for his support of the sophists, as well as for his dissolute desires. His house is the scene for both the *Protagoras* and Xenophon's *Banquet*.

"Who" I said, "and where and for how much does he teach?"

"Evenus" he said, "Socrates, from Paros, five minae."

And I deemed blessed Evenus, if truly he possessed this art and teaches at so modest a price. I, at any rate, would be preening myself on it, if I knew these things. But I do not know, Athenian men.   20c

Now, one of you might object: "But, Socrates, what is your affair?[13] From where did these slanders against you come? For surely if you were not engaging in anything any more than others, then such a rumor and account would not have been born, unless you were practicing something other than the many. Therefore, tell us what it is, lest we treat you rashly."   d

These things, it seems to me, are just—those the speaker says. And I shall attempt to show from whence this came, which brought to me this name and slander. Listen. Perhaps I will seem to some of you to be joking, but be assured, I will tell you the whole truth. For I, Athenian men, have received this name on account of nothing but a certain wisdom. What kind of wisdom is this? Perhaps that wisdom belonging to a human being. With respect to that, I probably really have this wisdom. Whereas, those of whom I just spoke, are by chance   e wise in either some wisdom greater than human wisdom, or some I don't know what. For I do not know it, and whoever says I do lies, and speaks in order to slander me. And, Athenian men, do not clamor against me, not even if I appear to you[14] to speak somewhat boastfully. For "not mine is the story"[15] which I will tell but I will attribute it to a speaker, an authority for you. For with respect to me, if I have any wisdom and of what sort, I will provide as witness to you the god in Delphi. You know Charephon,[16] surely. He was my companion

---

13 The word for affair is *pragma* and can also mean trouble or problem. In discussing Socrates, Nietzsche referred to the "Problem of Socrates".

14 The god in Delphi, Apollo, spoke in riddles about the destinies of men. The most famous pronouncement from the god was that Oedipus would kill his father and marry his mother. Oedipus tried to avoid his destiny and prove himself wiser than the Oracle by answering the riddle of the Sphinx, which is the riddle of man. He could not live with his knowledge, whereas Socrates' destiny constitutes his happiness.

15 Socrates uses the word *logos* for story, replacing Euripides' use of *mythos*. See *Symposium* 177a.

16 Charephon is Socrates' companion and admirer. In the *Clouds,* Charephon introduces Strepsiades to Socrates. The match ends with the destruction of both. Here we also see that Charephon is an eager admirer of Socrates who creates a bridge between Socrates and the *demos.*

21a   from youth and a fellow to many of you, and he shared your late exile
and returned with you. And you know what type Charephon was, so
fervent in what he would undertake. And once, indeed, having gone
into Delphi, he ventured to ask this of the oracle, and again I say—do
not clamor, men, for he asked if anyone was wiser than me. Then the
Pythia[17] answered that no one was wiser. And about these things his
brother here will give testimony to you, since the other has himself
reached his end.

b   Now consider the reasons for what I say, for I intend to teach
you from where the slander against me has come. For I, learning these
things, pondered thus: "Whatever is the god saying, and what riddle
is he speaking? As I, in fact, am conscious that I am not wise, either
much or little. Whatever, then, does he say when asserting that I am
wisest? For certainly, at the least, he is not speaking falsely, for that is
not decreed for him." And for a long time, I was at a loss about what
he even meant, then, very reluctantly, I turned to an investigation of
it something like this: I went to those opined to be wise, as there, if
c   anywhere, I would refute the divination and show to the oracle "that
this man is wiser than me, but you said I was wisest." Considering
this man, therefore, for it is not necessary to speak his name, he was,
however, one of the politicians, and considering him and speaking
with him, men of Athens, I received an impression something like
the following: it seemed to me that this man seemed to be wise to
many human beings and most of all to himself, yet he was not. Then I
attempted to show him that he thought he was wise but was not. From
d   this I became hated by him and by many of those present. When I went
away, I reasoned with respect to myself: "I am wiser than this human
being for it is likely that neither of us know anything noble and good,
but this one thinks he knows something while not knowing, whereas
I, as I do not know, do not think to know. At any rate, I am likely to
be a bit wiser than this one with respect to this peculiar thing—that
which I do not know, I do not think to know."

         From there, I went to another, one opined to be wiser than
e   him, and these things seemed to me the same. And from that point, I
incurred the hatred of both him and many others.

         After this, I went from one to another, perceiving, distressed,
and fearing that I was incurring hatred. Nonetheless, it seemed to be
necessary to hold the matter of the god as most important. Therefore,

17   The Pythia delivers Apollo's oracles.

to consider what the oracle meant, I had to go to all those reputed to know something. And by the dog, Athenian men, as it is necessary to   22a
speak the truth to you, I really underwent something like the following: the ones with the best reputations appeared to me to be nearly most deficient in my investigation in accord with the god, whereas others with paltrier reputations appeared to be men more suited to having prudence.

In fact, it is necessary to present to you my wandering as the doing of certain labors,[18] for the sake of the oracle becoming irrefutable. After the politicians, I went to the poets, the ones of tragedies and the ones of dithyrambs,[19] and the others, so that there I would lay hold   b
of myself in the act of being more ignorant than them. Therefore, I took up their poems that seemed to me they had worked on most, and questioned them about what they said, in order that at the same time I might also learn something from them. I am ashamed to tell you, men, the truth, nonetheless, it must be spoken. For so to speak, nearly all of those present could have spoken better about the poems than the ones who made them. Thus again with respect to the poets as well, I soon realized that they do not make what they make by wisdom but by some kind of nature and inspiration[20] like the diviners and deliverers   c
of oracles. For these also say many noble things, but they understand nothing of what they say. It was clear to me that the poets too are affected in the same manner. And at the same time, I perceived that they thought, because of their poetry, that they were the wisest of men in other things as well, in which they were not. Thus I left there too, thinking that in the end I was superior to them in like manner as I was to the politicians.

Finally, I went to the manual artisans, for I was conscious that I had knowledge, so to say, of nothing but surely I would discover   d
that they knew many noble things. And I was not deceived in this, for they knew of things of which I did not know, and in this respect were wiser than me. Yet, Athenian men, it seemed to me that the good craftsmen had failed in the very same manner as the poets. Since each one executed his own art nobly, he thought himself wisest and

---

18   Socrates here compares himself to Hercules whose labors were those of strength rather than of intellect.

19   A song in honor of the god of poetry Dionysus.

20   In Greek the word for enthusiasm literally means a god within. The poets were thought to have been inspired by the gods. The Muses are the daughters of Zeus.

worthy of other things—the greatest things, and this erroneous note
of theirs hid their wisdom. Thus I asked myself for the sake of the
e   oracle whether I would prefer to be just as I am, neither being wise at
all in their wisdom, nor ignorant in their ignorance, or to possess both
things they have. I answered to myself, and to the oracle, that it pays
me to be just as I am.

From this investigation, Athenian men, much hatred has come,
23a   the most grievous and serious kind, so that many slanders have arisen
from them, and I received this appellation of being "wise", for those
present at each occasion think that I am wise in those things about
which I refute others, whereas it is likely, men, that the god is wise, and
that the oracle meant that human wisdom is worth little or nothing.
And he appears to say this of Socrates and to have made use of my
b   name for the sake of making of me a pattern, as if to say, "the one of
you, human beings, is wisest, who, just like Socrates, realizes that in
truth, he is worth nothing in regard to wisdom."

Thus, up until now, I continue seeking and investigating, in
accord with the god, any townsmen or foreigner I think to be wise.
And whenever he appears to me not to be, I show that he is not and
come to the assistance of the god. And as the result of this occupation,
I have no leisure either to attend in a way worthy of speaking about
the affairs of the city or the affairs of my family. Rather, I am in ten-
c   thousand-fold poverty on account of my devotion to the god.

In addition to this, the young who voluntarily follow me, the
ones who have the most leisure—the sons of the wealthiest—delight
in hearing human beings questioned and often imitate me, and
themselves attempt to question others.[21] And, then, I think they find a
great many human beings who think they know something, yet know
little or nothing. Thence, the ones questioned by them are angry at
me, not themselves, and say that Socrates is someone most vile and
d   corrupts the young. And whenever someone asks them, "By doing
what and teaching what?" they have nothing to say but are ignorant,
and not to appear at a loss, they assert the things ready at hand against
all philosophers: "the things above and the things below the earth"
and "not believing in the gods" and "making the weaker speech the

21   In the *Clouds*, Socrates educates Pheidippides, who believes philosophy is a kind
of authority. He demands obedience to wisdom and is willing to claim the right to
punish his mother and father.

stronger."[22] For I don't think, they would wish to speak the truth, that in the end it is clear that they pretend to know while knowing nothing. Therefore, as they are, I think, ambitious and vehement and numerous, and as they have spoken of me in an orderly and persuasive manner for a long time, they have filled your ears.

e

From among these men, Meletus, Anytus, and Lycon attacked me. Meletus being angry on behalf of the poets, Anytus on behalf of the craftsmen and the politicians, and Lycon on behalf of the orators. Thus, as I said in the beginning, it would be a wonder to me, should I be able in so short a time to remove from you this slander which has grown to be so great. Athenian men, this is the truth for you. I am concealing from you nothing in my speech, either great or small, nor am I holding anything back, though I know well that I exact hatred from these very things, which is also proof that I speak the truth and that this is the slander against me and that these are its causes. And if you should investigate these things now or later, you will find it thus.

24a

b

So with respect to the things of which my first accusers accused me, let this be a sufficient apology to you. Against Meletus, however, the good and patriotic,[23] as he says, and the later accusers, I will attempt next to give a defense. Here again, as if they were any other accuser, let us take up their sworn statement. It is like this: Socrates, it says, does injustice by corrupting the young, and not believing in the gods in which the city believes, but rather in other, strange *daimonia*.[24] Such are the charges. Let us examine the charge in each of its particulars.

c

He says I do injustice by corrupting the youth, but, Athenian men, I say Meletus does, because he jokes with respect to a serious matter, readily bringing human beings to trial, pretending to be serious and earnest about matters for which he cared nothing at all. That it is thus, I will attempt to show you.

Now, come then, Meletus, and tell me: do you not consider how the youth will be the best possible as most important?

d

Meletus: I do

Soc: Come then, tell those men, who is it that makes them better. For

---

22   Aristophanes makes use of these prejudices to caricature Socrates.

23   Socrates here implies that Meletus is more imbued with hatred than with love and goodness.

24   *Daimonia* are certain bastard children of the gods, and, therefore, are appropriate go-betweens joining Socrates and the divine.

it is clear that you know, since you care. For having discovered the one who corrupts them, as you say, namely myself, you bring me before these men and accuse me. Come then, tell them and inform them who it is. Do you see, Meletus, that you are silent and have nothing to say? And does it not seem to you to be disgraceful and a sufficient proof of the very thing I say—that you never cared? Tell me, my good man, who makes them better?

Mel: The laws.

24e   **Soc:** But that is not what I am asking, best of men, but rather what human being is it who first of all knows this very thing—the laws.

Mel: These ones, Socrates, the judges.

Soc: How do you mean, Meletus? Are these ones here able to educate the young and make them better?

Mel: Most definitely.

Soc: All of them, or some of them and some not?

Mel: All.

Soc: You speak well, by Hera, and of a great abundance of benefactors. What then? The ones listening, do they make them better or not?

25a   **Mel:** Them also.

Soc: What about the councilmen?

Mel: The councilmen too.

Soc: Then, Meletus, the ones in the Assembly, the Assemblymen, they do not corrupt the young? Or do they also make them better?

Mel: Those as well.

Soc: Then it seems that all the Athenians make them noble and good except me; I alone corrupt them. Is this what you are asserting?

Mel: I do assert this most emphatically.

b   **Soc:** You charge me with a great misfortune. Now, answer me. Does it also seem to be the same to you with respect to horses? Do all human beings make them better, but one particular one is the corrupter? Or is it wholly contrary to this, that one particular one is able to make them better—or the very few who are skilled with horses, whereas the many, if they ever have to do with horses and use them, make them worse? Is it not thus, Meletus, with respect to both horses and all other animals?

It certainly is, whether you or Anytus deny it or affirm it. For it would be a great happiness for the young if one alone corrupts, and many other confer benefits. However, Meletus, you have sufficiently shown that you have never given any thought to the young, and you make clear your own lack of concern, as you care nothing for the things for which you have brought me to court.   c

But continue to tell us, Meletus, by Zeus, whether it is better to live with decent citizens or knaves. Answer sir, for I am asking of you nothing difficult. Do not knaves do something bad to those who are always near them, whereas the good something good?

Mel: Very much so.

Soc: Is there anyone, then, who wishes to be harmed by those he   d
is with rather than to be benefited? Answer, good man, for the law commands you to answer. Is there anyone who wishes to be harmed?

Mel: Surely not.

Soc: Come then, do you bring me here asserting that I corrupt the young voluntarily and make them more knavish, or involuntarily?

Mel: Voluntarily, I say.

Soc: What, then, Meletus, are you so much wiser at your time of life than me at mine, so that you know that the bad always do something bad to those nearest them, and the good something good, while I have come into so much ignorance as not to know that if ever I do   e
something vile to one of my companions, I will risk receiving in return something bad from him? And, yet, I do so much bad voluntarily, as you say? Of this I am not persuaded by you, Meletus, nor do I think is any other human being. But either I do not corrupt, or if I do corrupt, I do it involuntarily, so that in both cases what you say is false.   26a

And if I corrupt involuntarily, it is not the law to bring me here for such involuntary offenses but rather for you, in private, to take me aside and teach me and admonish me. For it is evident that if I learn, I will at least cease what I do involuntarily. But you fled being with me and teaching me, and were not willing, but you brought me here, where the law is to bring those who need punishment, but not learning.[25]

Thus, then, Athenian men, what I was saying is already evident—that Meletus never cared either much or little about these   b

---

25   Socrates here alludes to his belief that virtue is knowledge and vice is ignorance, or that punishment is against nature because it places blame where there is none.

matters. Nonetheless, tell us, Meletus, how do you mean that I corrupt the youth? Is it not clear from the indictment which you brought, that it is by teaching them not to believe in the gods in whom the city believes, but in other *daimonia* that are novel? Do you not say that by teaching these things, I corrupt them?

Mel: Certainly, I most emphatically do say so.

Soc: By these very gods, then, Meletus, of whom our discussion now is, speak to me and these men more clearly. For I cannot understand if you mean that I teach them to believe that there are some kind of gods—and thus that I myself believe that there are gods and am not myself completely without god,[26] nor do injustice in this respect, but that I do not believe in those in which the city believes, but in others, and this is your charge against me, that I believe in others. Or do you mean that I do not believe in any gods and that I teach this to others?

Mel: I say that you do not believe in gods at all.

Soc: O wondrous Meletus, on account of what do you say this? Do I not, then, as other human beings, even believe that the sun and moon are gods?

Mel: No by Zeus, judges, as he asserts that the sun is stone and the moon is earth.

Soc: Do you think you are accusing Anaxagoras, dear Meletus? And do you thus despise these men and suppose them to be so inexperienced in letters as not to know that the book of Anaxagoras of Clazomene is full of these accounts.[27] And, moreover, that the young learn these things from me, which they can purchase at times in the orchestra for a drachma at most; and, then, to mock Socrates if he were to pretend they were his own, especially since they are so atypical. But, before Zeus, is it thus I appear to you? That I believe there is no god?

Mel: Absolutely not, by Zeus, in no way at all do you believe.

---

26   The English word atheist comes from the Greek which literally means without God.

27   Anaxagoras was a natural scientist who was also the teacher of Pericles. When Socrates abandons his earlier way of looking at the world, he says that he was rejecting the thought of Anaxagoras (*Phaedo* 97b8-99d2). The fact that Anaxagoras' books are readily available suggests that Athens was more tolerant of science than Socrates suggests. According to Plutarch, Anaxagoras was charged with impiety and fled the city, but the charge was perhaps more the result of his relation to Pericles than of Anaxagoras' philosophy. Perhaps the charges against Socrates were more the result of his relations to Charmides and Critias than to his philosophizing.

Soc: You are unbelievable, Meletus, even to yourself, as it seems to me. For this man, Athenian men, appears to me to be very hubristic and unrestrained and simply to have brought this indictment with some sort of hubris, intemperance, and youthful rashness. He seems like someone testing me by composing a riddle: "Will Socrates the wise   27a know that I am jesting and that I contradict myself, or will I deceive him and the rest of the audience?" For he seems to me to contradict himself in the indictment, as if he should say, Socrates does injustice in not believing that there are gods and believing that there are gods. And surely this is the conduct of one who jests.[28]

Consider with me now, men, how he appears to me to assert this. And you answer us, Meletus. And you others, as I begged you at   b the outset, do not clamor if I speak in my accustomed way.

Is there any human being, Meletus, who believes that there are human affairs but does not believe that there are human beings?

Let him answer, men, and do not clamor incessantly. Is there anyone who does not believe that there are horses, but believes that there are affairs related to horses? Or anyone who does not believe in flute-players, but believes in matters related to flutes? There is not, O best of men. Lest you do not wish to answer, I speak to you and these others. But at least answer to this: "Is there anyone who believes in   c affairs related to *daimonia* but does does not believe in *daimons*?

Mel: There is not.

Soc: How helpful of you to answer reluctantly when compelled by these men. Now then, you assert that I believe in and teach things related to *daimons*. Therefore, whether old or new, according to your account, I do believe in things related to *daimons* and this you swore to in the indictment. But if I believe in things related to *daimons*, surely there is also much necessity for me to believe in *daimons*. Is it not thus? It sure is. I put you down as agreeing since you do not answer. But with respect to *daimons*, do we not believe they are gods   d or children of gods? Do you assert or not?

Mel: Much indeed.

---

28   Socrates believes that it is ridiculous for someone to believe in gods and not to believe in gods at the same time, which means that the gods exist or they do not exist. All thought that is theistic and atheistic is contradictory. Agnosticism appears problematic in this light.

Soc: Thus, then, I do believe in *daimons*, as you say, and if *daimons* are some kind of god, then it is this about which I say you riddle and jest: asserting that I do not believe in gods, though I believe in *daimons*.

But if *daimons* are certain bastard children of gods, either from nymphs or from some other of whom it is said, what human being believes in children of gods, but not in gods? For it would be strange, just as if someone believed in mules, children of horses or asses, but did not believe that there are horses or asses.

e

But Meletus, it cannot be other than that you brought this indictment either to try us in these things or because you were at a loss at what true injustice to allege against me. That you could persuade any human being, even one of little intelligence, that the same man believes there are things related to *daimons* and gods, and again that this same man believes in neither *daimons*, gods, nor heroes, there is no device.

28a

But in fact, Athenian men, that I do not do injustice according to the indictment of Meletus does not seem to me to need much of an apology, but sufficient even is this. And with respect to what I said earlier, that I have incurred much hatred and from many men, be assured this is true. This is what will convict me, if I am convicted, not Meletus, nor Anytus, but the slander and envy of the multitude. It has convicted many other good men already, and I think it will convict me as well. And there is no danger that it will stop with me.

b

Perhaps, then, someone might say, "Are you not ashamed, Socrates, for having engaged in the sort of pursuit from which you are now in danger of dying?" To that someone, with just words I would answer: "What you say is ignoble, fellow, if you think that a man, who is of even little use, ought to take into account the risk of living or dying, but ought to consider this alone when he acts: whether he is acting justly or unjustly and whether his deeds are of a good man or a bad. For according to your account, those who met their end at Troy would be contemptible, especially the son of Thetis. Instead of enduring anything shameful, he held danger in so much contempt that his mother, a goddess, spoke to him, something like this, I think, when he was ardent upon killing Hector; she says: "Son, if you revenge the death of your comrade Patroculus by killing Hector, thereupon, you yourself will die after Hector, destiny is upon you." He, on hearing this, made light of death and danger, dreading much more to live as a bad man and not avenge his friends. "Thereupon may I die," he says, "after

c

d

I inflict punishment on the doer of injustice, so that I may not remain here ridiculous beside the curved ships, a burden to the ground."[29] Certainly you do not think he gave any thought to death and danger?

Thus, in truth, it is, men of Athens. Wherever anyone stations himself, holding that it is best, or has been stationed by a ruler, there he must remain and face the danger, as it appears to me, and not take into consideration death or anything else in comparison to what is disgraceful. Thus I should have performed dreadful acts, men of Athens, if, when the rulers whom you elected to govern me stationed   28e
me in Potidaiea and Amphipolis and at Delium,[30] I remained where they stationed me and faced the danger of dying like everyone else, yet when the god stationed me, as I thought and assumed, ordering me to live the life of philosophy and to examine myself and others, I should then leave my station because I feared death and anything else   29a
whatsoever.

Dire indeed that would be, and then in truth someone might justly bring me to trial, asserting that I do not believe in the gods, as I would be disobeying the oracle, fearing death and thinking that I am wise when I am not. For to fear death, men, is in fact nothing other than to appear to be wise, while not being so. For it is to appear to know what one does not know; no one knows if death happens to be the greatest of all goods for a human being, but the multitude fear it as if they know well that it is the greatest evil. How is this not that   b
reprehensible ignorance, that of thinking that one knows what one does not know? But I, men, in this perhaps am also different from most human beings, and if I should assert that I am wiser than everyone in anything, it would be this: that as I do not know sufficiently about the things of Hades, I, therefore, also think that I do not know. But to do injustice and to disobey someone better than oneself, whether god or human being, I know is bad and shameful. Therefore, compared to the bad things which I know are bad, I will never fear to flee things that I do not know, which may even happen to be good, compared to the things I know are bad.

Thus, not even if you dismiss me now and disobey Anytus, who   c
claimed that either I should not have been brought here at all, or, since I was brought here, that it is impossible not to kill me, asserting to you

---

29   See *Iliad* Book XVIII, l.95-104.

30   In the *Symposium* (220d-221b), we are told that Socrates was courageous in retreat.

that if I am acquitted, soon your sons will be completely corrupted from pusuing the things Socrates teaches, and if you should say to me with respect to this: "Socrates, now we will not obey Anytus; we will allow you to leave, but on this condition—that you no longer pursue this investigation or philosophize, and if you are found still doing this, you shall die." If you should allow me to leave, as I said, on these

29d conditions, then I would say to you, "men of Athens, I welcome you and love you, but I will obey the god rather than you, and for so long as I breathe and am capable of it, I will surely not stop philosophizing, and I will exhort you and point out to any of you I happen to meet, saying the sorts of things I am accustomed to: "best of men, you are an Athenian from a city that is greatest and most renowned for wisdom and strength, are you not ashamed for being concerned with having as much as possible, as well as renown and honor, yet you have no

e concern for and give no thought to prudence and truth, and how your soul will be the best possible?" And if any of you debate it and say that he is concerned, I shall then not let him go and I will not depart, but will speak to him and question him and test him. And if he should appear to me not to possess virtue, but only says he does, I shall reproach him, saying that he holds the things worth the most as least

30a important, and the pettier things as more important. I will act thus to anyone I meet, younger or older and both foreigner and townsman, but especially the townsmen as you are closer to me in kin.

Let it be known that god commands this. And I think that until now no greater good has befallen the city than my service to the god. For I go about doing nothing other than persuading you, both

b young and old, not to care for bodies and money as earnestly as how your soul will be the best possible. I say, "Virtue does not come from money, but from virtue comes money and all the other good things for human beings both private and public."[31] If by saying these things I corrupt the youth, then it might be harmful. But if anyone says that what I speak is other than this, he speaks without sense. With respect to these things, Athenian men, I would say, either obey Anytus or not, and either let me go or not, since I will not do otherwise, even if I were to die many times.

c   Do not clamor, Athenian men, but stick to what I asked you and do not clamor at the things I say, but listen. For, as I think, you

31 Socrates thought that only the philosopher loved virtue, whereas others need to be taught that money will come from virtue. The idea is paradoxical since Socrates is poor.

will benefit from listening, as I am going to tell you other things at which, perhaps, you will clamor, but do not do so on any account. Rest assured that if you kill me, being the man that I say I am, you will not harm me more than yourselves. For neither will Meletus nor Anytus harm me, he would not even be able to, for I do not think it is possible for a better man to be harmed by a worse. Perhaps he may 30d kill, or banish, or dishonor me, and this man no doubt, and others as well, think that these are great evils, whereas I do not think so, but much rather to do what this man is now doing—trying to kill a man unjustly.

Thus, I, Athenian men, am far from making an apology on my behalf, as one might think, but I do it on your behalf, lest by condemning me, you do something wrong with respect to the gift the   e god has given to you. For if you kill me, you will not easily find another of my kind, who, though it may sound absurd to say, has simply been set upon the city by the god, as upon a great and well-born horse that is somewhat slow, because of its great size, and needs to be awakened by a gadfly, so the god seems to have set me upon the city as such a one. I awaken and persuade and reprove every one of you, and I do 31a not cease besetting you the whole day. Men, another of this kind will surely not arise easily for you. Thus, if you obey me, you will spare me. But perhaps being irritated like the drowsy when they are awakened, you might obey Anytus and slap me, easily killing me. Then you would live the rest of your life in sleep, unless the god, in his care for you, sends you someone else.

That I happen to be someone of this kind, given by the god to the city, you may discern hence: it does not appear to be human to   b have neglected all my own things and to have endured that the affairs of my family be neglected for so many years now, whereas I always attend to your business, going to each of you in private, like a father or older brother might, persuading you to the concern for virtue. If I was benefiting from this, and receiving pay for my exhortations to these things, there would be some explanation, but it is the case, you yourselves see, that even the accusers, who shamelessly accused me in all other things, have not been able to become so completely shameless   c as to bring in a witness to testify that I ever took money or asked for it. For that I speak the truth, I think I offer a sufficient witness: my poverty.

Perhaps, however, it might seem to be strange that, going around being a busybody in private, I give this counsel, but do not dare go

before your multitudes to counsel in public. The reason for this is the one you have heard me tell many times and in many places, that
31d   something divine and daemonic comes to me, a voice that Meletus, making a comedy of it, mentioned in the indictment. This began with me in childhood, a sort of voice comes, and whenever it does, it keeps me from whatever I am about to do, but never urges me on.

This is what opposes my participation in politics, and this opposition appears to me to be entirely noble. For be assured, men of Athens, that if long ago, I had attempted to be politically active I would long ago have perished, and would have benefited neither you
e   nor myself. Do not be angry with me for speaking the truth. For there is no human being who will be spared from either you or any other multitude, should he be single-mindedly opposed to and prevent many unjust and illegal things from taking place in the city, but it is
32a   necessary for one who really fights for the just to lead a private, rather than a public life, in order to preserve himself even for a brief time.

I will offer to you great proofs of this, not speeches but what you honor, deeds. Listen, then, to what has happened to me, that you may see that I would not yield to one man against the just on account of fear of death, though I would perish for not yielding. I will tell you vulgar things, common to the law courts, yet true. For I, Athenian
b   men, never held any office in the city but that of Councilman. And it happened that my tribe Antiochus constituted the prytany[32] when you wanted to judge as a group the ten generals, the ones who did not rescue the men from the naval battle, against the law as it appeared afterward to all of you.[33] Then, I alone of all the prytanes opposed you doing anything against the laws and I voted against you. And though the orators were ready to indict me and arrest me, and you were ordering and urging them on, I thought that I should face danger with
c   the law and the just on my side rather than like you, who on account of fear of prison or death, were counseling unjust things.

---

32   A prytany is an administrative period. There were ten a year corresponding to each of the tribes, whose councilmen, selected by lot, served as prytanes.

33   The generals abandoned the dead and left some of the living for dead. According to Homeric poetry, these men were lost souls because they were never put to rest. The demagogue Theramenes aroused religious fear and indignation, as well as democratic jealousy against the generals, who were put on trial together, convicted, and executed. See Xenophon, *Hellenica*, I 7.

And this was when the city was still ruled democratically. But when it became an oligarchy, the Thirty[34] sent for five of us to the Tholos,[35] and ordered us to arrest Leon the Salaminian and bring him from Salamis for execution.[36] And they ordered many others to do many things of this kind, wishing that as many as possible would be implicated in the criminal charge. Then, however, I showed once more, not in speech but in deed, that I do not care about death, if it   32d is not too rude to say, in the slightest way, but that all my care was to do no unjust or impious deed. For that government, as strong as it was, did not terrify me into doing anything unjust, but upon coming out of the Tholos, the four went to Salamis and arrested Leon, but I went home. And I might have died because of this, if that government had not soon been destroyed. And of these things you will have many   e witnesses.

Do you think, then, that I would have survived so many years, if I had been in public affairs and had acted in a way befitting a good man, aiding the just things, and as one ought, considering this as most important? Far from it, Athenian men, nor would any other human being.

But I, throughout my entire life, if I was ever publicly active, it   33a is apparent that I was the kind of man, and I was the same in private, who never conceded anything to anyone contrary to justice—neither to those my slanderers say are my students, nor to anybody else. I have never been the teacher of anyone, but if anyone desired to hear me speaking and going about my business, whether young or old, I never refused it to him. Nor do I converse only when I receive money,   b and not when I do not receive any, but to rich and poor alike I give myself to questioning, and if anyone wishes to hear what I say, he can

---

34   "The Thirty" refers to the oligarchs instituted by the Spartans at the end of the war. Among these were Critias and Charmides, with whom Socrates had some relation. His association with them, as well as with Alcibiades, might have encouraged the charges and indictment. Anytus, who Xenophon presents as the most vengeful of the accusers, was exiled during the brief reign of the Thirty, only to return as one of the leaders of the democracy. Xenophon suggests that Socrates' association with Alcibiades and Critias was the reason for the charge of corrupting the youth (*Memorabilia* I.2. 12-48).

35   The meeting place of the prytanes under the democracy.

36   Leon of Salamis was reputed for his justice, which no doubt stood as a reproach to the Thirty. They hoped to implicate as many as possible in his murder in order to spread the blame and soften the outrage. Socrates uses the example of Leon to shed some light on his own trial and conviction.

respond to me. And with respect to these, if any one of them becomes an upright man or not, I cannot be justly held responsible, because I have neither promised them any instruction nor taught them any. If anyone ever says that he learned from me or heard in private anything that anyone else had not, be sure that he does not speak the truth.

But why do some delight in spending so much time with me? You
33c   have heard it, Athenian men! I have told you the whole truth—that they delight to hear those examined who think they are wise but are not, as it is not unpleasant. I have been commanded to practice this by the god, as I say, by divinations, and by dreams, and by every means that any divine decree ever commanded a human being to do anything at
d   all. These things, Athenian men, are both true and easily tested. For if I am corrupting the youth now, and have already corrupted others, and if any of them, having become older, recognized that I even advised them badly in anything when they were young, then now, surely, they should have stood up to accuse me and take revenge for themselves. If they themselves were unwilling to do it, some of their families (fathers and brothers, and other relatives) should now have recalled it and taken revenge, if their families had suffered anything bad from me.

However, there are present here many of them whom I see: first
e   Crito here, my contemporary and my deme, the father of Critobulus here; then Lysanius the Sphettian, the father of Aeschines here; then there is Antiphon the Cephisean, the father of Eigenes. In addition, here are others, whose brothers have kept time in this manner: Theozotides' son Nicostratus, the brother of Theodotus—Theodotus has died so he could not beg him to stop, and the son of Demodocus Paralus, whose brother was Theages. And here Adeimantus son of
34a   Ariston, whose brother is Plato here, and Aeantodorus whose brother is Apollodorus here.

I could mention many others to you, some of whom Meletus particularly ought to have offered as a witness in the course of his own speech. If he forgot, let him now offer one, I will give way to him and let him speak if he has anyone of the kind. But totally to the contrary of this, you will find, men, that everyone is ready to assist me, the
b   corrupter, who does evil to their families as Meletus and Anytus say. Those who have themselves been corrupted might have a reason to come to my assistance, but those who have not been corrupted, the relatives, men of older years, what other reason can they have to assist me except the correct and just one, that they know Meletus speaks falsely whereas I am being truthful?

Well then, men, these and perhaps other things are pretty much the things I have to say in my defense. Perhaps some among you may be indignant upon recollecting himself, if he should have, in contesting   34c a trial even smaller than this trial, begged and supplicated the judges with many tears, bringing forward his children and many other of his relatives and friends, in order to be pitied as much as possible, whereas I will do none of this, despite that in this as well, I might appear to be risking the greatest danger. Perhaps someone thinking about this may become rather set against me, and being angered by this very thing, he might set his vote down in anger, should there be anyone of you like this. I, however, do not think that there is, but if there is, it seems to me   d decent to say to him, "I, best of men, do indeed have some relatives", for it is just as Homer says: "not even have I sprung from an oak or a rock but from human beings,"[37] so that I have a family and sons too, three of them, Athenian men, one now a youth and two still children. I will, nonetheless, not bring them forward to beg you to vote to acquit me.

Why, then, will I not do this? Not because I am stubborn, Athenian men, nor because I disrespect you. Whether or not I am   e undaunted by death is another matter, but with respect to reputation, mine and yours, and the whole city's, it does not appear to me noble for me to do any of these things as I am old and have this name, whether true or false, it is repeated at least that Socrates is different from the   35a generality of human beings in some manner.

If those among you who are reputed to excel, whether in wisdom or courage or any other virtue whatsoever, should act in such a manner, then it would be shameful. I have often seen some who, when brought to judgment, though reputed to be something, do wondrous deeds, as thinking they will suffer something dreadful if they die, and as if they would be immortal if you did not kill them. They seem to me to disgrace the city, so that a foreigner might suppose that those Athenians who excel in virtue, whom they choose from   b among themselves for their own public offices and other honors, are no better than women. For those of you, Athenian men, who are reputed to be something in like manner, you should neither do these

---

37   In *Odyssey* XIX. 163 and *Iliad* XXII. 126 this phrase is used by Penelope and Hector, respectively, to connect our identities and emotions to our origins. Socrates' Delphic mission, to the contrary, encourages an attachment to truth and reputation contrary to sentimentality. His care for his sons is to make sure that they are stung with questions like every other citizen.

things, nor, whenever we do them, should you allow it. But you should make manifest that you would much rather vote to convict him who introduces these piteous dramas and makes the city look ridiculous, than him who stays silent.

35c
Reputation aside, men, it does not seem to me to be just to beg the judge, or to be acquitted through begging, but rather to teach and to persuade, for a judge does not sit to hand out justice as a favor, but to judge, as he has not sworn to favor whoever seems likeable to him, but to judge according to the laws. Therefore, we should not accustom you, and you should not be accustomed, to making false oaths, as neither of us would be pious.

d
So do not think that I, Athenian men, ought to practice such things toward you which I consider to be neither noble, nor just, nor pious, as well, by Zeus, certainly not when I am being accused of impiety by Meletus here. For clearly, if I should persuade you and force you through begging, having sworn an oath, I would be teaching you that there are no gods, and while making my defense speech, would accuse myself of not believing in gods. But that is far from being so, for I believe, men of Athens, as none of my accusers do, and I give it to you and the god to judge me in the manner that is best both for me and for you.

[*A vote is taken and the majority finds him guilty. Meletus proposes the death penalty and Socrates offers a counter proposal.*]

e
36a
There are many concurrences, men of Athens, that keep me from being indignant at this outcome, that you voted to condemn me, and one of them is that the outcome was not unexpected by me. I, however, wonder at the number of votes on either side, as I did not think that [the vote] would be by a few but by many. But now it appears that if only thirty votes had fallen otherwise, I would have been acquitted. So far as Meletus is concerned, it seems to me that I have already been acquitted; and not only have I been acquitted but it is clear to all that, had not Anytus and Lycon come forward to accuse me, he would have to pay a fine of a thousand drachmas, as he would not have obtained a fifth of the votes.

b
As is the case, the man proposes for me the penalty of death. Well now. What shall I in return propose to you, men of Athens? Is it not clear that it should be that for which I am worthy? What is it, then? What do I deserve to suffer or pay because during my life I remained quiet and did not care about the things for which the many care—money and the household, and military command and popular

oration, as well as the other offices, and the conspiracies and factions that grow in the city—as I considered myself too decent to survive   36c if I took part in these things? I did not enter into affairs where, if I entered, I would be of no benefit to either you or to myself, but to each of you I went in private to do the greatest benefaction, I affirm, and I endeavored to persuade each of you not to care for anything of his own before having cared for himself—how he will be the best and most prudent possible, and not to care for the things of the city before having cared for the city itself, and to care for other things in the same manner. What penalty, then, do I deserve, being as I am?   d Something good, men of Athens, at least if you give me what I deserve according to my true worth—and, moreover, a good of a kind that would be fitting for me. What then is fitting for a man of poverty, a benefactor, and one who needs leisure to exhort you? There is nothing more fitting, Athenian men, than that such a man be given his meals in the Prytaneum,[38] and much more fitting than if any one of you won a victory at Olympia with a horse or a chariot, either two or four horse. For such a one makes you seem to be happy, whereas I make you so;   e and he does not need sustenance, but I am in need. Therefore, it is necessary for me to propose what I deserve consistent with justice. I propose then to be awarded my meals in the Prytaneum.

Perhaps, however, in proposing this, I seem to you to speak   37a in almost the same proud manner as I spoke about lament and supplication. But it is not the case, Athenian men, but rather that I am convinced that I do not voluntarily do injustice to any human being, though I have not persuaded you, as we have conversed with each other for but a short time. You would be persuaded, as I suppose, if you had a law like other human beings, not to try someone in a matter of death in one day alone, but over many. But as things stand, it is not   b easy to erase great slanders in a short time.

Being convinced, then, that I do not do injustice to anyone, I am far from doing injustice to myself by declaiming against myself, that I myself deserve something bad, and by proposing this sort of thing as my desert. What should I fear? That I might suffer what Meletus proposes for me, to which I say that I do not know whether it is good or bad. Instead of this, should I choose something of the things I know well to be bad, and propose that? Should I propose prison? And why should I live imprisoned, a slave to the authority that is

---

38   Meals at the Prytaneum were reserved for the greatest benefactors of the city.

37c   regularly established there, the Eleven?[39] Or should I propose money
and imprisonment until I pay? But for me this is the same penalty of
which I just spoke, as I have no money to pay.

Should I then propose exile? For perhaps you would allow me
this as my desert. I should indeed have much love of soul, men of
Athens, if I were so unreasonable as not to be able to see that you,
who are my fellow-citizens, have been unable to endure my way of
d   life and speeches, but rather that they have become burdensome and
hateful to you, so that you now seek to be free of them—will others
then easily bear them? Far from it, Athenian men. Fine indeed would
life be for me, a human being of my age to be exiled going from city
to city, always being driven out. For I know well that wherever I might
go, the youth will listen to me when I speak, as they do here. And if I
repel them, they will themselves drive me out, persuading their elders.
e   But if I do not repel them, then their fathers and families will drive me
out on account of these same youths.

Yet, perhaps someone will say: "Socrates, can you not live in exile
from us, by being silent and keeping quiet?" This is the hardest thing
of all of which to persuade some of you. For if I say that it would be to
disobey the god, and on this account it is impossible to keep quiet, you
38a   will not be persuaded by me, supposing that I am being ironic. If, on
the other hand, I say that this is a very great good for a human being—
to make speeches every day about virtue and other things of which you
have heard me speak when examining myself and others, and that for
a human being the unexamined life is not worth living, still less, when
I say these things, will you be persuaded by me. Yet, such is the case, as
I affirm, men, however to persuade you is not easy.

And at the same time I am not accustomed to think of myself as
deserving something bad. If I had money, I would have proposed as
b   much as I could afford to pay, since that would do me no harm. But it
is the case that I do not have any money—unless of course you want
me to pay what I am able. Perhaps, then, I could pay you a minae of
silver. So I propose that amount.

But, Plato here, Athenian men, and Crito, Critobulus, and
Appolodorus urge me to propose thirty minae and they will guarantee
it. So I propose that amount and they will be sufficient guarantors of
the money for you.

---

39   Socrates is speaking of the eleven prison authorities, chosen by lot from the
citizenry.

[The jury votes to condemn Socrates to death]

    You, in order to save a little time, men of Athens, will get a   38c
reputation and be charged with the guilt of having killed Socrates, a
wise man, by those wishing to defame the city. For those who wish
to defame will assert that I am wise even if I am not. In any case, if
you would have waited a short time, this would have taken place on
its own. You surely see my age, that it is far advanced in life and close
to death. I do not say this to all of you, but to those who voted to
condemn me to death.

    And I say this as well to these same persons. Perhaps you think,   d
men of Athens, that I have been convicted for want of the kinds of
speeches that would have persuaded you, as if I had thought that I
should do or say anything to escape the penalty. Far from it. I have
been convicted for a want, not of speeches, but of boldness and
shamelessness, and willingness to say the kinds of things to you that
would have pleased you most to hear—to have me wail and lament   e
and do and say many other things unworthy of me, as I affirm, but
such as you have been accustomed to hear from others. But neither
then did I think that I ought to do anything, in order to avoid danger,
unworthy of a free man, nor do I regret having defended myself as I
did. I would much prefer to die defending myself like this than to live
like that.

    For neither in a trial nor in a war should I or anybody else plan
to escape death by doing anything possible. In battle it is frequently   39a
evident that one might escape death by laying down one's arms and
turning to supplicate one's pursuers. And, there are many other
devices in every danger to avoid death, if one dares to do and to say
anything. But I suspect this is not difficult, men, to avoid death, but
that it is much more difficult to avoid wickedness, for it runs faster
than death. And now I, being slow and old, am taken by the slower   b
of the two, but my accusers being clever and agile, are taken by the
faster—wickedness. And now I leave, condemned by you to death, but
they are by the truth convicted of wretchedness and injustice. And I
abide by my sentence, as do they. These things, perhaps, must be as
they are, and I suppose there is just measure in them.

    Next, I desire to prophesize to you, O you who voted to condemn   c
me. For now I am where human beings are apt to prophesize, when
they are about to die. I say to you who have condemned me to death,
that vengeance will come to you straight away after my death, and

far more severe by Zeus, than the kind you have given me by killing me. For you have done this thinking you will be freed from giving an account of your life, but rather quite the contrary will happen to you, as I affirm. There will be more who will confound you, whom I have been restraining though you did not notice them. And they will be more severe in so far as they are younger, and you will be angrier. For if you think that by killing human beings you will keep someone from reproaching you for not living correctly, then you do not think finely. For that kind of escape is neither at all possible nor noble. But rather the noblest and easiest kind is not to restrain others, and to prepare oneself to be the best possible. Having foretold these things to you who voted to condemn me, I am set free.

d

e

40a

b

c

But with you who voted for me, I would gladly converse about what has taken place, while the officials are busy and I do not yet go to the place where, when I do go, I must die. Stay with me, men, for this time. Nothing keeps us from telling stories to one another for as long as possible. For I am willing to show you, as to friends, the meaning of whatever it is that has just occurred to me. To me, at least, judges, and by calling you judges I address you correctly, something wondrous has happened. For my customary prophesy from the *daimonion* was always very frequent on all other former occasions, opposing me even in trifling matters if I was about to do something wrong. But now you yourselves behold what has happened to me, which anyone might think to be, and which is believed to be, the ultimate evil. Yet, when I departed from my home this morning, the sign of the god did not oppose me, nor when I came up here to the trial, nor anywhere in my speech when I was about to say anything, despite that in other speeches it has frequently restrained me while I was talking. But now, with respect to this proceeding, it has not opposed me, in either deed or speech. What, then, do I think is the cause of this? I will tell you. It is likely that what has befallen to me is good and that it is not possible that those think correctly who think being dead is bad. To me, a great proof of this has occurred, for it is not possible that the accustomed sign should not have opposed me, unless I were about to do some good.

But let us keep in mind the following possibility in which there is a great hope that it is good. For being dead is either of two things. It is either like being annihilated and the dead man has no perception of anything, or as it is said, it is a kind of change and passage of the soul from here to another place.

And if there is no perception, but it is like a sleep in which the   40d
sleeper has no dream whatsoever, death would be a wondrous gain.
For I think that if someone had to pick the night in which he slept so
soundly that he did not even dream, and had to compare the other
nights and days of his life to that one, and then upon reflection had
to compare how many days and nights in his own life he had lived
better and more pleasantly than that one, then I think that, not just a
private man, but the Great King himself would find them easy to count   e
compared to the other days and nights. Now, if death is something like
that, I at least say it is a gain, as in this manner, all time seems to be
nothing more than a single night.

On the other hand, if death is like a journey from here to another
place, and if what is said is true, that all the dead are indeed there,
what greater good could there be than that, judges? For if arriving in   41a
Hades,[40] released from those here who claim to be judges, discovering
judges in truth—the very ones who are said to judge there—Minos
and Rhadamanthys, and Aeacus and Triptolemus, and those other of
the demi-gods, who were just during their own lives, would this be a
paltry journey? Or again, how much would any of you give to be with
Orpheus and Musaeus and Hesiod and Homer? I, indeed, am willing
to die often, if these things are true, as for me in particular, passing   b
time there would be wondrous. I would compare my own experiences
with theirs when chancing upon Palamedes,[41] or Telemonian Ajax,[42] or

---

40   Socrates is taking issue with the account of Hades given by Odysseus (*Odyssey,*
      Book XI). A comparison between these two accounts provides insight into Plato's
      intention.

41   Palamedes, whose name means literally a "handy or contriving man," was one of
      the Greek heroes in the Trojan war depicted in the tales after Homer. His tragedy
      was treated also in plays by Aeschylus, Sophocles, and Euripides, all now lost.
      The myth about him varies, although it runs generally as follows. Odysseus had
      feigned madness to avoid joining the Greeks in the Trojan war, but the clever
      Palamedes disclosed his ruse by means of a test: he either placed Odysseus' infant
      son (Telemachus) in Odysseus' path while he was pretending to plow his field
      dementedly, or he threatened to kill the infant with a sword. Odysseus saved his
      son, thereby revealing his sanity. Odysseus then contrived a plot to murder him
      in revenge: he forged a letter from Priam to Palamedes that promised a payoff
      in gold if he were to betray the Greeks; he then buried the identical amount in
      Palamedes' place at camp. After reading the letter, Agamemnon discovered the
      gold and delivered Palamedes into the hands of the army, who stoned him to death
      (cf. Apollodorus, *Epitome* 3.7-8; Hyginus, *Fabulae* 95.2, 105). He is mentioned
      especially for his proverbial cleverness. (See in particular Euripides, *Orestes* 432;
      Aristophanes, *Frogs* 1448-52.)

42   Ajax committed suicide.

anyone else of the ancients who died on account of an unjust verdict. And I think it would not be unpleasant.

And in particular the greatest thing, to spend time examining and discovering those there, as I do to the ones here, whoever of them is wise and whoever thinks he is but is not. What would one give, men of the jury, to examine the one who led the great army against Troy,

41c   or Odysseus, or Sisyphus, or the thousand others whom one could mention, both men and women, with whom to converse and to be with and to examine would be inconceivable happiness? Certainly those there do not kill for that. For they are happier than those here, in other things as well as being deathless for the rest of time, provided the things said are true.

But you, men of the jury, should also be of good hope toward death and to hold in mind this certain thing as true—that for a good

d   man there is nothing bad, whether alive or dead, neither are the gods without care for that one's troubles, nor have my current troubles come from themselves, but it is clear to me that it is now better for me to be dead and to have been freed from my troubles. On account of this, the sign did not turn me aside, and I am neither in any way angry at those who voted to condemn me, nor my accusers. Though it was not with this in mind that they voted to condemn me and accused me, rather

e   they thought to harm me. For this, they deserve to be blamed.

This much, however, I beg of them. Punish my sons when they grow up, men, paining them as I have pained you, should they appear to you to care for money or anything else more than virtue. And if they are reputed to be something, though being nothing, reproach them as I have you—that they do not care for the things they should and that they think they are something when they are worth nothing.

42a   And if you do these things, we will have been treated justly by you, I myself and also my sons.

But now it is time to depart—I to die and you to live. Which of us takes a better path is unclear to everyone except the god.

Xenophon's *Apology of Socrates to the Jury*

[1]   But Socrates, it seems to me, is worthy of being remembered also for the way, after being summoned to appear before the public tribunal, he deliberated with himself both concerning his defense speech and the end of his life. Certainly there are others who have written about this, and all have had the occasion to mention his arrogant boasting[43] —which shows clearly that Socrates delivered the speech in just that way. However, that he had already come to think death was more choice-worthy for himself than life— *this* they have not brought out clearly at all. And so it appears, therefore, that his arrogant boasting was very imprudent.

[2]   Hermogenes, on the other hand, the son of Hipponicus, was his companion, and has spread such reports about him as make it appear that his arrogant boasting suited his intention. Indeed, this fellow reported that when he saw Socrates conversing about everything else other than the trial he said,

---

43   In the choice for the phrase "arrogant boasting" as a consistent translation of *megalēgoria*, I go somewhat further than previous translations. Treddenick translates it inconsistently as "arrogant tone," and "haughtiness" which imply a certain petulance or snobbery. Patch translates it as a "boastful manner of speaking", which seems to me too weak. As Patch indicates, the word means literally "talking big". It is a very rare term. But a comparison between the kinds of contexts in which this word is found (both in Xenophon and elsewhere) is revealing of a crucial ambiguity – especially in light of the charges brought against Socrates. In Aeschylus (*Seven Against Thebes*, 50-5) and Sophocles (*Antigone*, 1347) the term is used for that kind of arrogance associated with cruelty, tyranny, and impiety, and is hated by the gods; in all cases it is spoken only by the choruses as defensive accusations, including in Euripides (see *Children of Heracles*, 356). In the *Anabasis*, Xenophon uses it to refer to certain men who might be humbled by some divinity for their "arrogant boasting" (*Anabasis*, 6.3.18). In the *Agiselaus*, however, it is used more to refer to a vice in one's relation with other men, a human defect (not seen in light of giving offense to the gods), and is there opposed to good graces (*eucharis*). (Dionysis of Hilicarnasis' use of the term in reference to the character of Thucydides' style does not justify the meaning "high minded" or "lofty" speech, as Fielding and Dakyns translate it. See *On Thucydides*, 27) See also *Cyropaideia*, 4.4.2, 7.1.17.

[3]   "Socrates, shouldn't you now be considering too what defense you plan on delivering?" Socrates reportedly at first answered the charge, "Do I not seem to you to have lived my whole life caring for my defense speech?" But when Hermogenes reportedly asked, "How is that?", Socrates allegedly stated, "Because I went through life committing no injustice, and this, I believe, is the noblest way to take care of my defense speech."

[4]   Yet, when Hermogenes allegedly replied back, "Don't you see that Athenian juries, when they are irritated by arguments, often condemn to death those who have committed no injustice, while just as often they have acquitted doers of injustice, when persuaded by pitiful or charming speeches?", Socrates reportedly declared, "Yes, of course. But, by Zeus, it happened already twice that when I tried to consider my defense the *daimonion* thwarted me."[44]

[5]   When, however, Hermogenes reportedly said, "You tell of wonders!" Socrates supposedly again answered the charge: "So you believe it a wonder if it seems better to the god too that I die now? Don't you know that until now I have not conceded to anyone that he had lived better than me? It is surely very pleasing for me to know I have lived my entire life in holiness[45] and justly; and, moreover, while admiring myself greatly, I also discovered that those who spend their time with me recognize these same things about me."

[6]   "Now, however, if my age is extended further still, I know it will be necessary to pay the penalties of being old: seeing and hearing getting ever worse, and learning with ever greater difficulty, I will forget even what I have learned. If I then become conscious of my deterioration and reproach myself, how can I," he reportedly said, "continue to live pleasantly?"

[7]   "But you, see here," he reportedly declared, "the god, too, out of his benevolence may very well be preparing a release from life for me, not only at the proper moment, considering my age, but in the easiest manner. For if I am condemned now, clearly I will be able to procure for myself the death

---

44   Aristotle states in the *Rhetoric* [2.23.8]: "Another topic is derived from definition. For instance, that the *daimonion* is nothing else than a god or the work of a god; but he who thinks it to be the work of a god necessarily thinks that gods exist. ...In all these cases, it is by definition and the knowledge of what the thing is in itself that conclusions are drawn upon the subject in question." Aristophanes' Socrates never mentions any prophetic or warning *daimonian*, not even before the secret education of Strepsiades.

45   In regard to a respectful disposition towards the gods, Xenophon uses the words *hosion* and *eusebios*, which will always be translated as 'holy' and 'pious' (and their derivatives) respectively.

judged easiest by those whose duty it is to take care of this, one both least troubling to friends, and which engenders the greatest longing for the dead.[46] For whenever one leaves nothing disgraceful[47] or disagreeable behind in the thoughts of those close to him, but rather, with a healthy body and a soul capable of affection, fades away–isn't it necessary that he will be sorely missed?"

[8]   "So the gods were correct when they thwarted me from considering the speech," he reportedly said, "while it then seemed to us that we must search out every means to obtain an acquittal. For if I had succeeded in doing that, rather than now taking leave of life, clearly I would have been preparing for myself a death afflicted by suffering from illnesses, or old age, whither all difficulties flow together, a time utterly devoid of cheerfulness."[48]

[9]   "By Zeus, Hermogenes," he reportedly said, "I will not be zealous for those things, but for the opinion I have of myself, and of as many noble things as I believe I happened upon, coming from both gods and humans. And if I incense the judges by bringing *that* to light,[49] I shall choose to die rather than to remain alive slavishly, begging in order to win a far worse life instead of death."

[10]   And with such decisions, Hermogenes said, when his accusers brought the charges against him—that 'he did not believe in the gods the city believed in, but that he introduced other strange divinities, and corrupted the young,' he reportedly came forward and said:

[11]   "I am, however, struck with wonder, men, firstly at this charge from Meletus, what on earth he can be thinking of when he states that I don't believe in the gods the city believes in; because, just as everyone else who happened to be there saw me sacrificing during the communal festivals, at least, and at the public alters, Meletus himself too could have done so, if he had wanted to."

[12]   "How can I be introducing truly strange *daimonia* when I say the sound of a god appears to me, giving signs as to what must be done? Surely the others too conjecture from the signs in sounds, whether they use the cries of birds or the utterances of humans. And who will argue with thunder,

---

46   Compare the disposition of Aristophanes' Socrates toward the question of suicide in the *Clouds*, 775 ff.

47   The word *aschēmōn* means both shameful and ugly, just as *kalon* means both noble and beautiful.

48   The last phrase of this sentence reads like a profound saying from the poets.

49   Following the unexpected and difficult reading with the mss. *tautēn* (referring to *doxan*, "the opinion").

that it is either a sound or an enormous omen? And then there's the priestess on the tripod at Pytho:[50] doesn't she herself convey in sound messages from the god?"

[13]   "But surely, that the god is prescient of what shall immanently come to pass, and grants premonitions to whomever he wishes, so this too, just as I assert, everyone says as well as believes.[51] Yet, while they give the forebodings names like 'birds,' or 'utterances,' or 'signs,' or 'prophets,' I, on the other hand, call this '*daimonion*'. And in so naming it, I think, I speak more truthfully and in a more holy way than those attributing the power of the gods to the birds. In fact, I have this too as evidence that I definitely don't tell any lies about the god: although I proclaimed to many of my friends what the god's counsels were, I never yet appeared to be lying."

[14]   When the judges reportedly heard these things they clamored loudly, some disbelieving what was said, while others were actually envious, that greater things even from the gods had happened to him than to themselves; and Socrates reportedly spoke back to them: "Yes, come on! Hear these other things too, so that whoever among you wants may disbelieve still more in my being honored by *daimones*. For at some time or other, when Charephon inquired about me at Delphi, while many were present, Apollo ordained in response that no human was freer, more just, or more moderate than I."

[15]   Now on further hearing these things the judges reportedly clamored even more loudly, as is probable; and so Socrates, reportedly, spoke again: "And yet, men, the god pronounced in oracles greater things about Lycurgus, the lawgiver for the Lacedaemonians, than he did about me. For it is told how he himself directly addressed him who was entering the temple, saying, 'I AM CONTEMPLATING WHETHER TO SAY YOU ARE A GOD OR A HUMAN.'[52] But

---

50   Socrates refers to "Pytho" which is a particular surname, the only one used by Homer, for the Delphian Apollo. It recalls the specific deed of Apollo by which he was given this name. Apollo had slain the serpent Python which inhabited the caves of Mount Parnassus. Two sections later Socrates will refer to the same holy place as "Delphi." The tripod Socrates mentions was a sacred throne from which the sitting priestess, after performing a mysterious ceremony, pronounced sounds interpreted into words and prophetic utterances by priests.

51   Socrates makes a clear distinction between saying and believing.

52   Cf. Herodotus, *Histories* 1.65.1. Xenophon subtly alters the quotation from the source. Herodotus makes the Pythia speak the following verses:
    O Lycurgus, you have come to my lavish temple,
    You, beloved of Zeus and of all who have a home in Olympus,
    I am in doubt whether I shall prophesy that you are a god or a human,
    Nevertheless, I have even more hope that you, Lycurgus, are a god.

he didn't compare me to a god,—although he did select me for being superior to many humans.[53] Nevertheless, you should not believe the god heedlessly, even regarding these things. You should, rather, consider carefully each and every one of the things the god said."[54]

[16] "Now then, whom do you know that is less of a slave to their bodily desires than I? Or, whom do you know among humans more free than I, I who accept neither gifts nor pay from anyone? Or, whom would you likely[55] believe more just than one so in harmony with his present condition that he needs not a single additional thing from the possessions of others. And how could one plausibly fail to say that I am a man who is wise, I who from the very moment when I began to be aware of things spoken, have never yet ceased to seek out and learn whatever good was in my power?"

[17] "And doesn't this seem to you evidence I haven't toiled uselessly: many citizens who strive for virtue, as well as foreigners, choose out of all the rest to associate with me? And what shall I assert is the cause of this: that while all know I would be the least likely to have the means to repay them, many, nevertheless, desire to present me with some gift? Or of this: that not a single one reclaims benefactions from me, but many instead agree that they owe me thanks?"

[18] "Or of this: during the siege,[56] while others were pitying themselves, I went through the ordeal with no greater hardship than when the city enjoyed the pinnacle of its good fortune?[57] Or of this: that while others procure for themselves luxuries from the marketplace at great expense, I, on the other hand, produce without cost stuff of the soul more pleasant than those things? Now assuredly, if in what I have claimed about myself nobody could convict me of lying, how, then, could I fail to be justly praised by both gods and humans?"

[19] "So then, Meletus, do you nevertheless claim that I corrupt the young by intentionally doing these kinds of things? Indeed, we surely understand what corruptions of the young are. So speak, if you know anyone who, because of me, went from piety to unholiness, or from moderation to insolent pride,[58] or from thrift to prodigality, or from moderate drinking to being a

---

53   Or, "selected me to be superior." It is ambiguous whether the god's election is the cause or the effect of Socrates' superiority.

54   The intentional ambiguities in the Greek in §§15-16 are worth noting. The 'divine' utterances can probably be interpreted in different ways.

55   Or *fairly, equitably.* (*eikotōs*)

56   Cf. *Hellenika* 2.2.10

57   "Good fortune" here, may also be rendered as "happiness" (*eudaimones*).

58   *hubris*

drunkard, or from loving labor to soft laziness, or who was overcome by some other wicked pleasure."

[20]   "Yes, by Zeus," Meletus declared, "I do, however, know those whom you persuaded to obey you rather than their fathers who begat them." "I do admit it," Socrates reportedly stated, "at least where education is concerned. For they know I have taken care to study the matter. But where health is concerned humans obey doctors rather than parents. Also, in the public assemblies, to say the least, all the Athenians, surely, obey those who speak most prudently rather than their relatives. Indeed, don't you also choose as generals in preference to fathers and brothers—Yes, by Zeus! in preference even to yourselves— those whom you think most prudent in matters of war?" "It is so, Socrates," Meletus reportedly stated, "because it is both advantageous and customary."

[21]   "Well then," Socrates reportedly said, "doesn't even this seem a wonder to you: that in other affairs the strongest do not get merely an equal share, but are preferred in honor, while I, because I was selected by some as best in what concerns the greatest good for humans—education—on account of this, I am being prosecuted by you as warranting the death penalty?"

[22]   Now clearly much more than this was said by him and by his friends who joined him in his cause. I, however, did not seriously intend to state everything pertaining to the trial. Instead, I was satisfied to make clear that, while Socrates wanted then,[59] above all, to give the appearance of having committed neither any impiety against the gods, nor any injustice against humans,[60]

[23]   yet, he also didn't think he ought to plead earnestly to avoid death; but he himself believed it was then the proper time to die. And it became still clearer that he understood the situation in this way after the vote delivered a verdict against him. Firstly, when he was ordered to propose the alternate punishment,[61] he would neither do so himself, nor allow his friends to do so. On the contrary, he said that to propose an alternate punishment would be admitting one had committed an injustice. Later, when his companions wanted to abduct him, he didn't go along with them, but actually seemed to be mocking when he asked them whether they in fact knew of some place outside of Attica inaccessible to death.

---

59   Following Patch's reading *tote*, and with the manuscript.

60   Dakyns goes out of his way to try to give alternate renderings for this phrase all of which seem more acceptable to his sensibilities. Treddenick follows this path, and Todd departs from it only partially. Patch also shies away from a literal rendering.

61   This was the practice according to the Athenian law in such cases.

[24]   Furthermore, when the trial was coming to an end, Socrates reportedly said, "To be sure, men, those who instructed the witnesses that they ought, while breaking their oaths, to testify falsely against me, along with those who obeyed them, are all necessarily conscious of their own great impiety and injustice. Why, however, is it now fitting for me to think any less of myself than before I had been judged guilty—considering I was not proven to have done anything for which they prosecuted me? For I have not appeared to sacrifice to or swear by strange *daimones* instead of Zeus, Hera, and the gods among them, nor to believe in other gods."

[25]   "How, too, could I have truly corrupted the youth by habituating them to fortitude and frugality? Moreover, certainly regarding acts for which the punishment of death is established—temple-robbery, burglary, selling freemen into slavery, and treason—not even do my accusers themselves claim I have committed any of them. So to me, at least, it seems a wonder how on earth my deed warranting death was shown to you."[62]

[26]   "No, surely not because I am being killed unjustly, ought I, because of *that*, to think any less of myself. No indeed, this is not shameful for me, but for those who have condemned me. Moreover, Palamedes,[63] who died in a way similar to me, also gives me encouragement. For even up until now he is the source of far nobler hymns than is Odysseus, who murdered him unjustly. I know that the future, just as the times gone by, will testify that I never committed any injustice against anyone, nor ever made anyone worse. On the contrary, it will testify that I gratuitously benefited those conversing with me, by teaching whatever good was in my power."

[27]   After saying these things, he left in a manner so much in agreement with what he had said before: there was cheerfulness in his eyes, his bearing, and his gait. And the moment that he noticed those escorting him were crying he reportedly said: "What's this? Are you only just now starting to cry? Have you really not known for a long time already that from the day when I was born a death sentence was voted by nature against me? Now if, as it stands, I am to be annihilated prematurely, while good things are

---

62   Stobaeus had made a correction of the text of the manuscript (in the *Florilegium*). The manuscript reading is difficult to accept; Marchant, Todd, Dakyns, and Treddenick all follow this emendation. Patch comments on the difficulty but does not follow the manuscript. I see no reason to depart from what Xenophon wrote, which is prepared for in §§ 13, 16, 22, and 24 above.

63   See note 39. Xenophon has Socrates referring to the tragedy of Palamedes elsewhere (*Memorabilia* IV.2.33): " 'In the affairs of Palamedes too, have you not heard about his suffering? Indeed, they all, in fact, sing hymns telling how he was killed by Odysseus, because he was envied for his wisdom.' – 'These things are also told,' he [Euthydemus] said."

continuing to flow, obviously I as well as those who feel good will towards me should be grieved. If, on the other hand, I am being released from life just when the severest difficulties are expected to come, then I suppose every one of you ought to be cheerful, considering that all is going well for me."

[28] But, then, a certain one of those present, Apollodorus, who was, though powerfully attracted to Socrates, in other respects a simpleton, said: "Still, Socrates, what is hardest of all to bear, for me anyway, is that I have to watch you being put to death unjustly." It is said that Socrates, stroking Apollodorus' head, replied: "Would you, dearest Apollodorus, wish to see me put to death justly rather than unjustly?" And with that he supposedly laughed in a kind way.

[29] It is also told that when he saw Anytus[64] passing by he said, "Now there is a man full of glory,[65] as though he had accomplished something great and noble by killing me, all because when I saw the city considering him as worthy of the greatest offices, I declared that he shouldn't educate his son to be a tanner." "What a base wretch he is," he declared, "he doesn't seem to know that whichever of us has accomplished the more useful and nobler things for all time, that he is also the victor."

[30] "Besides this," he reportedly declared, "just as even Homer ascribes foreknowledge of things that shall happen[66] to some who are on the verge of fading from life, I too wish to prophesy something. I was, at one time, briefly acquainted with Anytus' son, and to me it seemed he didn't have a weak soul.[67] I declare, therefore, that he shall not remain in the slavish occupation his father has arranged for him; but, since he hasn't any earnest guardian, he will fall victim to some shameful desire, and will surely descend further into a base wretchedness."

[31] And in saying these things he didn't lie; in fact, the youth was delighted by wine, and he did not stop his drinking by night or day. So in the end he became worthy of nothing, neither for his city, nor for his friends, nor for himself. And though Anytus has since died, it is actually because of his son's debased education and his own bad judgment that he has still got a bad reputation.

---

64   Cf. *Hellenika* 1.2.18, and 2.3.42-44.
65   Here "full of glory" translates *kudros*, a very rare term also implying exalted pride; nearly always ascribed only to gods and divinities or those close to them. However, see also Xen., *Art of Horsemanship* Ch.10 §§15 & 16.
66   Cf. *Iliad*, 16.851-861
67   The term *arrōstos* can mean both "sick" and "weak".

[32]   On the other hand, because Socrates boasted of his own greatness[68] while in court, and thereby brought envy upon himself, he made the judges vote to condemn him all the more. To me, therefore, it seems he met with a fate loved by the gods. Indeed, while he left behind life's severest difficulties, he also met with the easiest of deaths.

[33]   He demonstrated, too, the strength of his soul. For as soon as he discerned that being dead was better for him than to be still alive – just as he was not averse to other good things – he did not weaken in the face of death; on the contrary, he gladly accepted it, and brought it upon himself.

[34]   And truly, when I reflect on the wisdom and the inborn nobility [69] of the man, I can neither fail to remember him, nor to remember him without praising him. If, however, anyone among those striving for virtue has been with someone more advantageous than Socrates, I believe that man is most worthy of blessedness.[70]

---

68   The term *megalunein* recalls the opening theme of Socrates' *megalēgoria*.

69   The root word, *gennaios* (well-born, noble), is the same as that used by Plato to describe the lie given at the founding of the city in the *Republic* (cf. 414c; and 375a, 409c).

70   The term *axiomakariotatos* seems to occur but once in all of Greek literature. All previous translators, including L.& S., have rendered it "worthy *to be deemed* most blessed." I have chosen to follow the direct meaning of all similar compounds with *axio-* , and to omit the "deemed" from the translation.

Interpretive Essay: Plato and Xenophon

Introduction

Plato's *Apology of Socrates* is a drama that justifies the life of philosophy and challenges the authority of the pagan gods, heroes, and the poets who celebrated them. This means that the trial of Socrates is poetry in defense of philosophy. It is an act of reformation that brings a new divinity into the city.

The introduction of Socrates as a heroic and even divine being had far-ranging effects. The universality of both Christianity and of the Enlightenment would be unimaginable without his example. This is not to argue that Socratic philosophy is either Christian or modern, but rather that Socrates prepared the break with the ancient city, its gods, and heroes, which made possible the authority of both an otherworldly god and of modern science. From the Socratic perspective, however, these are temptations and errors.

The far-ranging effects of Socratic wisdom gave birth to Socrates' latest accuser. Nietzsche argued that Socrates was the greatest corruptor, not only of the Athenian youth but of mankind. He placed Socrates in history as the destroyer of the pagan world, and as the first cause of both the Christian and the Enlightenment traditions. The defining Socratic duty—his Delphic mission to know himself by questioning others, was, according to Nietzsche, an expression of plebian resentment. Socratic dialectic belongs to the stage of human decay where the traditions and gods of the nobles no longer inspire and where there is need for new ends or limits. Reason promised that end, but in so far as it is dialectical, it only issues forth in critical resentment and in low-minded concerns for utility.

Socratic wisdom, in its non-critical aspect, is ascetic. The philosopher sacrifices the gods for the truth, for an abstraction, for a stone. This new form of ascetic dedication prepares Christianity and its rational counterpart, science. The combination of the plebian and the ascetic constitutes modern

39

life, and in this way, Socrates is the cause of the modern world and the pollution of man. Nietzsche abandoned reason as nihilistic and advocated the will to power.

As Nietzsche knew, the Socrates whom he is criticizing is Plato's. Xenophon's Socrates is not dialectical and otherworldly. He was in no way plebian and ascetic, and played little to no role in the inspiration of Christianity, science, and democracy.

Xenophon, like Nietzsche, destroys the tragic appearance of Plato's *Apology*. In Xenophon's *Apology*, the conflict between Socrates and the city is a subplot in the greater drama of his relation to Hermogenes, a private man who aspires to be a gentleman. Gentlemen are men of practical affairs, who need books and especially history and historical biography to educate them in their ways. In general, Xenophon's Socrates appears as an advisor or counselor, and hardly seems philosophic, especially when compared to Plato's Socrates. Xenophon's Socrates does not reveal convention for convention, and moreover, he is not Xenophon's only hero. Xenophon presents Cyrus as an admirable alternative. Xenophon makes a completely different appeal for philosophy and consequently established a completely different tradition from Plato. From Xenophon emerged the heroic tradition of Plutarch with its reflections on the virtues and vices of great historical men seen in light of gentlemanly virtues. Xenophon refuses to allow philosophy to cast a shadow of darkness over the city, its heroes, and its gods. Plato, however, made his Socrates the unambiguous peak of human existence and allowed him to stand triumphant over the city as a god of light over a dark cave. If we are to understand the difference between Plato and Xenophon we must grasp why Plato thought it necessary to present Socrates in the light he did.

Plato's *Apology*

I. The Delphic Oracle and the Meaning of Wisdom

In order to defend himself against the charges of impiety and of corrupting the youth, Socrates presents himself as a lover of the true religion and as the true example of piety, whereas the city and its education corrupts. He says that he must defend himself, not only against his immediate accusers like Meletus, Anytus, and Lycos, but also his judges, who are prejudiced against him, for he has gained a reputation as a wise man or one who investigates the things above and beneath the earth, and who makes the weaker speech the stronger. The judges have been prejudiced against him by accusers of old, who have long since died, and who slandered Socrates to the current citizens from the time they were children. In brief, Socrates asserts that the education of the citizens is one of unthinking prejudice handed down to them from their forefathers.

Aristophanes, in his *Clouds*, where Socrates is shown to be both a natural scientist and a teacher of rhetoric, is the only one of the slanderers who can be named. This means that Aristophanes is a thinking critic. Socrates broadens the base of his accusers in order to challenge the city as a whole and in order to engage the most thoughtful criticisms of him. He makes his defense more difficult in order to address the most respectable and challenging opponents. Only in this manner, can he accomplish his apology.

Socrates introduces the story of the Delphic Oracle in order to explain the source of hatred against him. Charephon asked the Delphic Oracle if anyone was wiser than Socrates. The Oracle answered that no one was wiser. Socrates, in humble fashion, doubted the oracle and set out to refute it, only to discover that he was in fact the wisest of men. His inclination was not to believe in the Oracle, and only to agree with it once he had shown his own superior wisdom to himself. In other words, it is his own reason that is his guide. The Oracle must pass before him, rather than he before it.

Socrates also appears humble and pious because he only has knowledge of ignorance, but this knowledge of ignorance, or human wisdom, is really a claim to the only possible wisdom. Claiming knowledge of ignorance is so far from being humble that it is a statement meaning that one knows the character of ignorance as it manifests itself in others. Those others are natural scientists, sophists, politicians, poets, and manual artisans. To grasp the peculiar character of their ignorance is to grasp the peculiar character of Socratic knowledge.

The natural scientists, like Socrates, are suspected of impiety because they study the places inhabited by the gods—the things above and beneath the earth. They claim to have knowledge of the macroscopic and microscopic, and consider this knowledge to be knowledge of the whole or comprehensive knowledge. Socrates does not deny that it would be impressive to have this knowledge, but he denies that either they or he has it. No one has this knowledge of the whole, because it is impossibly founded upon a misconceived notion about the whole. The natural scientist only studies that part of nature that is body and motion. He cannot comprehend the universe insofar as he is related to it, because the human is outside of his view.[71]

---

71   The image of the divided line and of the cave in the *Republic* make clear the limitations of natural science. The philosopher who tries to study nature directly, as if it were a homogenous whole, is blinded. In terms of knowledge, the study of natural science is redeemed only as a step towards political philosophy.

The blindness to what is human is itself a human defect requiring explanation. Natural science is above all a human activity, through which the natural scientist practices a form of self-forgetting. He finds security in his dedication to knowledge, but he has not examined the meaning of this dedication. In fact, his dedication makes no sense in light of his own understanding of nature because body and motion are meaningless and unworthy of dedication. He practices a form of asceticism whereby he tries to avoid facing his own existence by subordinating himself to his science. The whole is inextricably related to human beings and how they live, and a failure to explain this relation is a failure to examine the whole. Because the scientist lacks self-knowledge, he lacks knowledge of the whole, which is really knowledge of the relation of parts.

The self-forgetting of the scientist is paradoxically a form of self-sacrifice and, therefore, contains a religious instinct. But, this instinct is in contradiction with science itself. His life and his science are in contradiction, and his unwillingness to face it is the mark of his ignorance.

The rhetoricians are also an example of ignorance. They believe that argument is an art for gaining victory. They teach that justice is only conventional or by human agreement. Rhetoric or persuasion is the most important art or form of knowledge because it can be used to persuade assembled men and to manipulate the law for one's own benefit. The rhetoricians go from city to city selling their art, living outside of country and above law.

The rhetoricians claim to be able to educate human beings or to understand the end or perfection of a human being and how to bring that end to fruition. They respect speech and enjoy the reputation for being wise, yet they also teach for money and hold it in high esteem. Furthermore, the lesson that justice is only conventional and that by nature man wants to tyrannize is in conflict with the rhetorician's own self-respect, because he believes that he practices an art of a very high order. As the materialism of the natural scientist is in conflict with his own activity, so too the art of the sophists is in conflict with their own lives. Neither can live with their own beliefs.

Moreover, the sophists neither teach, nor know the art of war despite the fact that they do not believe in justice. They believe that money is real and offers security, and on top of that, it confers respect. They have no real sense of the abyss that they proclaim. They talk tough but are weak and conventional.

The politicians and the poets are also given as examples of ignorance. It was by questioning them in particular, rather than the natural scientists and sophists, that Socrates became hated. He questioned those politicians reputed to be wise and refuted them with the consequence of becoming hated to both them and those with them. Socrates says of the politicians that they were of the opinion that they knew what was noble and good even though they did not, which makes them more ignorant than Socrates, for if Socrates does not know something he claims not to know.

The claim to know the noble and the good is different from the claims to knowledge made by the natural scientists and the sophists. The scientists claim to have knowledge of physical nature, and the sophists claim to have knowledge of an art, whereas the politicians claim to know man's duty. They are leaders, and as such are capable of a reputation for wisdom, but not wisdom itself. The politician and his followers reinforce one another in a community of belief; the former believing himself wise because others think it and follow him, and the latter believing him wise because they are flattered by him. The politician does not have knowledge, but the ability to inspire obedience and confidence, which is really not leading but being led since the politician must speak to the passions of his audience. Socrates pulls the rug out from under this mutual support group to show that they are just feeding upon one another.

Next, Socrates spoke to the poets. They claim to have inspired knowledge of the divine, and it is the divine that traditionally serves as a guide for knowledge about the noble and the good. Socrates says that when questioning the poets, he realized that almost everyone else would have spoken better about the poetry of the poets than the poets themselves, even though the poets made the poetry themselves. Socrates suggests that, ultimately, the people are the authority for the poet, because the poet writes for them.

After making the allusion to the authority of the audience over the poet, Socrates says that the poet makes what he makes not out of some kind of wisdom but by some sort of nature, and while inspired, like diviners who give oracles. Like diviners, the poets say many noble things but know nothing of what they speak. In order to grasp the error peculiar to poetry, the comparison of poets to diviners must be examined in light of the allusion to the authority of the audience. The diviners do not know what they say, but, nonetheless, have a reputation for being wise because they flatter the audience's desire for divine knowledge of the future. Both the politicians and the poets are examples of the error of self-indulgence, or of ordering the world around man's own neediness. The politicians lead men against others, while the poets protect men from a godless universe.

The ignorance of which Socrates speaks last is that of the manual artisans. They actually do possess some real knowledge. The knowledge of the mechanical arts is universal and teachable. The gods and the laws differ from city to city; the knowledge of natural science is not real because it is capable of infinite revision; and rhetoric is really nothing more than the art of persuasion through either logical argument or the talent for moving the passions of the many. The knowledge, however, characteristic of carpentry, for example, can be practiced everywhere and is demonstrable to all regardless of agreement. Despite this, Socrates says he would rather remain ignorant in his own way than to have the know-how or expertise of the artisans.

Even the artisans themselves are dissatisfied with their knowledge, since on the basis of it, they pretend to greater kinds of knowing. Their competence in the arts leads them to believe that they could be authorities in human affairs, but their capacity as artisans provides no knowledge of human affairs. In fact, the mechanical arts have nothing to say about human beings, and, therewith, of the artisan himself. The artisan asserts his supremacy, but the arts do not provide the basis for such an assertion and even deny its possibility. The knowledge characteristic of the manual arts is really a form of self-forgetting ignorance, to which the artisan is blinded by the pride and comfort of his own practical expertise.

These examples of error or of kinds of ignorance point to the meaning of human wisdom. Human wisdom would have to be free from the various self-indulgences as well as the various self-forgettings. It is by understanding what philosophy is not, that we can begin to understand what it is.

II. Socrates and Meletus: Philosophy and Authority

Meletus, on behalf of the poets, accuses Socrates of not believing in the gods of the city and of corrupting the youth. Anytus and Lycos later step forward to support Meletus—the former two on behalf of the politicians and artisans, respectively, and the latter on behalf of the orators. Meletus is the main accuser and he draws attention to the fundamental dependency of the ancient city and its laws on poetry and the gods.

Traditionally, when one is accused of crimes against the city and its gods, one begs pity. No matter how high-born, one sheds tears, gets down on one's hands and knees, and brings out one's family to supplicate the jury. The Athenian court is really like the stage of a tragedy with the jury sitting like an audience and hoping to be flattered by a spectacle of tears.

Socrates, however, does something novel. He says that he will speak as he is accustomed, which means that he will cross-examine his accuser in the dialectical manner characteristic of the Platonic dialogues. He will bring to the city the doubts of philosophy instead of tragic fear and pity.

The examination of Meletus is part of Socrates' substitution of the ancient gods and heroes with philosophy. Upon questioning, Meletus asserts that the laws, the judges, the councilmen, and pretty much everyone but Socrates make the youth good, because everyone else educates the youth to respect for ancestral authority. Socrates then introduces the example of horses and other animals, asserting that the few who know the art of training make them better. The example of horses and other animals refers back to an earlier distinction between human beings and citizens. A human being is natural, whereas a citizen is artificial or conventional. Human beings belong to nature, whereas citizens belong to their particular city and its beliefs. These are two different kinds of beings with different educations. Socrates claims to be interested in the former kind of education and suggests that the latter is a corruption.

Socrates then accuses Meletus of being one of the many who have given no consideration to the education of the young, suggesting that Meletus' real concern is not with the souls of the young, but with preserving the authority of those the young must obey. Socrates argues that, if he makes people worse, he does so out of ignorance and deserves to be educated instead of punished.

The law uses force to confirm the mind, rather than argument, and for this reason is *the* very example of self-indulgent error by which Socrates characterized the politicians and the poets. Socrates equates vice with ignorance and virtue with knowledge, implying that the laws are corrupt, since they punish with a view to vindicating authority.

In addition to accusing Socrates of corrupting the youth, Meletus accuses him of not believing in the gods of the city, and instead believing in other strange gods. He goes even further by accusing Socrates of being an atheist or one totally without god. Socrates denies that he is an atheist by asserting that it is Anaxagoras who said that the sun is just a stone, leaving open the question of whether or not Socrates agrees with Anaxagoras.

The conversation with Meletus about the gods is itself an example of the new Socratic poetry that awakens by exposing the weakness of one's reason. Meletus contradicts himself by saying that Socrates both believes in gods (strange or foreign gods) and does not believe in any gods whatsoever. The awakening of awareness through contradiction makes Socrates hated.

Yet, this form of reasoning is not strange to Athens, and is not even entirely strange to the courts, for we know that the rhetoricians practiced it. What is new and strange is that the practitioner of this reasoning should be elevated above the gods and heroes, and establish new standards for virtue and vice. Socrates reforms the rhetorical schools by sublimating argument towards philosophy.

Socrates says that Meletus is laughable and that his accusation belongs in a comedy, thereby raising the question of whether or not that is where it in fact is. Aristophanes' *Clouds* ridiculed Socrates for his way of life, but the Platonic comedy laughs at those who contradict themselves, and everybody lives in contradiction except for Socrates. The ridiculous contradiction to which our thought is drawn is to both believe and not to believe in gods at the same time. Either the gods exist or they do not exist. If they do not exist, it is ridiculous to want them to exist, for that would be to believe in the gods and not to believe in the gods. There is no possibility of atheistic theism and of theistic atheism.

In response to the ridiculousness of believing and not believing in gods, Socrates supposes that someone might make the following objection: that Socrates ought to be ashamed of himself for embarking on a course that will now bring him to his death. The objection assumes that capital punishment ought to create shame—that the authority of the law and of the judges ought to be respected because they hold the power of life and death. Socrates refuses to allow his mind to be determined by his desire for security or his fear of death, and it is his peculiar relation to death that makes his life different from the lives of all other human beings.

In order to prove his freedom from the distortions caused by the fear of death, Socrates compares himself, of all people, to Achilles, who was the greatest of the Greek heroes, and who died young for the sake of glory. The wrath of Achilles is the subject of the *Iliad* and Socrates takes up this subject by examining Achilles' revenge against Hector on behalf of Patroculus. Socrates claims that Achilles feared ridicule. In other words, the fear of being belittled lies behind his wrath, rather than any noble and just passion.

It is not difficult to see that Achilles is to Hector as the city is to Socrates. As Achilles wants to affirm the meaning of his friendship to Patroculus by killing Hector, so the city wants to vindicate itself against Socrates because he takes from it what is dearest to it; and what is dearest to it is its belief in its own eternity. The city looks ridiculous through the eyes of Socrates, because it builds prejudices to protect itself.

Underneath the need for eternity and the fear of ridicule is the fear of death. Through the glory of his deeds, Achilles gives up his life in order to hold on to it. His desire for eternity is, in the eyes of Socrates, nothing more than an error stemming from the fear of becoming nothing. Socrates is not shamed by the opinion of others any more than he is shamed by death. He says that "to fear death is to seem wise but not to be so." This is a Socratic riddle about wisdom just like the "knowledge of ignorance". They are really two ways of expressing the same thing.

Socrates does not fear death because he does not know whether Hades is the greatest evil or the greatest good. He certainly does not seem to think Hades is terrifying on account that it cannot be known. What he does know is that philosophy is the greatest good and that the unexamined life is not worth living. Anytus told the jury that since they have indicted Socrates, they now have no other choice but to convict him, as he will corrupt the youth if he is allowed to continue philosophizing. Socrates tells the jury that if they were to let him go on condition that he no longer philosophize, he would refuse since he would rather obey the god than them. He will continue to exhort to concern for the soul rather than riches, reputation, and honor. He is so far from being a corruptor that he is a gift, given to Athens as a gadfly to a lazy horse. His questions inflict the pain of doubt, but they bring men closer to nature. The city can crush him at its will, but it will have destroyed its greatest benefactor.

Socrates and the *Daimonion*

Socrates raises the paradox of being a benefactor dedicated to the city who never sought to involve himself in public affairs, but instead went to each person in private. The solution to this paradox is his *daimonion*, which is a voice that restrains him from pursuits that threaten his life, and, according to Socrates, the public pursuit of justice, rather than the private pursuit of it, would have killed him in short order.

After having stated that his *daimonion* preserves him, he discusses the public deeds he did perform. He argues that these deeds are examples of his heroism, or of his willingness to risk his life for justice. One wonders how heroic these deeds could have been if his *daimonion*, which preserves him, allowed him to perform them. The first deed belongs to the democracy, and the second to the oligarchy. The democracy placed on trial together, and put to death together, the generals at Arginusae for failing to recover the bodies of the dead lost at sea. According to Greek poetry, these souls, never having been put to rest, are haunted for all eternity. The horror of their suffering prepared popular outrage. In the face of religious terror and indignation, Socrates advocates obedience to the laws with no specification as to those laws. After executing the generals, the democracy repented, thinking that what it had done was unlawful.

The second example of Socrates' political activity is his disobedience to the oligarchy. He was ordered, with four other men, to arrest Leon of Salamis, but Socrates went home while the others arrested Leon, who was then executed without trial. Socrates says that his disobedience might have cost him his life, if the oligarchy had not soon been overturned. Both the democracy and the oligarchy persecute in accordance with their dominant passions: the former from religious terror and the latter from fear of the people.

In comparison to the courage expected of every Athenian citizen, Socrates' political deeds could only appear impressive to a coward. The mind behind the deeds is truly impressive. He was free from the passions that gripped each party. That does not mean that he never felt the fear for his own life, but that he never allowed that fear to distort his mind. The threat of public life is less a threat to preservation than to the preservation of one's mind, for many Athenian politicians were capable of surviving politics.

In both the case of the democracy and of the oligarchy, Socrates not only does what is just but what is safe for himself. What could be safer in a democracy than to advocate the law? His disobedience to the oligarchs was in tandem with their weakness. Had he served them, he might not have survived the incoming democracy. It would seem that when forced to be a part of politics, his concern is with surviving so that he can live another day to philosophize. Socrates' famous *daimonion*, no less than the Delphic oracle, proves to be an argument for the superiority of his own judgment and of the life of philosophy.

On the day of the trial, the *daimonion* did not speak to Socrates. He interprets its silence as a sign that now is a good time for him to die. When he was young, he sought to fulfill his nature, and now when he is old, he is ready to die. If he were young would he provoke the jury and refuse to beg for his life? The *daimonion* is consistent with his own judgment.

Socrates says to the jury that if they had waited a little longer, nature would have killed him, but since they have decided to, they will have to face the questions of his followers, whom he had restrained, and who will no doubt be angry with the city for having killed him. The jurors are mistaken if they think that by killing him, they will avoid having to given an account of their own lives. His questions are more unrelenting than the jealousy of

Hera, and unlike Io, there will be no rest for the city from its gadfly. His sting will outlive him.

Despite having followers, Socrates denies that he is a teacher. He did not promise instruction and did not take money for it. He cannot help it if the young enjoy watching those who think they are something revealed to be nothing. His activity of questioning, while infuriating to authority, has an undeniable charm for some youth.

He knows that the jury will hate him. Other men, for lesser offenses, have begged pity, even bringing their families before the court. Socrates appears stubborn and proud for not bending down on his knees and crying, which is what the jury wants from him. It judges with its pity rather than the law, and when its pity is not satisfied, it judges with its hatred.

Pity and hatred are passions in need of restraint. Pity affirms one's superiority in a gentle manner and hatred in a violent manner. These two passions can temper one another, but Socrates would rather see both restrained by judgment in accordance with the law. He says that the man who comes begging before the judges brings shame not only upon himself but upon Athens, since it is unmanly to beg and since the judges have sworn before Zeus to uphold the law and not their feelings. He appeals to a certain prejudice on behalf of manliness to reform the court culture.

Socrates is found guilty and is given the opportunity to propose a counter-penalty to death. He is not surprised by the verdict, but he is surprised by the narrow margin of the majority. It is apparent to him that he has some support from the jury and that there is no clear agreement with Meltus' proposal to kill him. His counter-proposal must be read in light of the fact that he knew there was a good chance to avoid the sentence of death.[72]

For Socrates, his sentence is a question of what he deserves, and what he deserves is to be supported in his life of philosophy by the city. Since he is poor and in need of leisure, they should feed him, and not just anywhere, but in the Prytaneum. After all, the Olympic victors who are fed there only seem to make the citizens happy, whereas Socrates really makes them happy.

He knows this is an outrageous request and follows it up with an explanation of why he did not propose prison, a fine, or exile. He will not propose to do injustice to himself, as if he were deserving of something bad,

---

72   Strauss argues that Plato's Socrates is similar to Xenophon's to the extent that both are committing suicide. Leo Strauss. *Studies in Platonic Political Philosophy* (University of Chicago Press, 1983) p. 53.

and he will not propose something bad for himself in order to stay alive, when he is not sure if dying is good or bad. The spirit of skepticism, and one might say agnosticism, since we are speaking about skepticism in relation to questions of death, is a reasonable appeal to the irrational. The agnostic appears to exercise his judgment by not being able to judge. Socrates lends his example to make this position seem intellectually respectable, and by doing so moderates the court. He says that if the Athenians had a law like other human beings, not to judge in a matter of capital punishment in one day but over many, then he could have persuaded them of his innocence, but it is not possible for him to do away with great slanders in a short period.

Socrates emerges as a new and more ambitious Athena. She won over the vengeful furies by allowing them to protect the city, whereas Socrates attempts to moderate patriotism by enlisting the sense of right on the side of philosophy and of wrong on the side of the city. In this sense, the *Apology* is a correction to the *Oresteia*, or an attempt to go further than Aeschylus towards bringing reason to the city. In the *Apology*, dedication to the city seems so far from civilizing man that the prosecution of the laws appears as persecution.

Socrates does not propose imprisonment for himself, because he would have to endure the authority of the Eleven. Exile would be bad because he is an old man, and would have to endure going from city to city, for he will not stop philosophizing, and he can hardly expect foreigners to accept his questioning when his fellow citizens find him intolerable. He will not stop philosophizing because the one thing he does know is that it is a very great good for a human being to make speeches every day about virtue and about the other things of which he converses, and that the unexamined life is not worth living.

He did not propose a fine because he has no money, yet after having insulted the jury as men whose lives are not worth living, he then proposes a fine of one mina. He even proposes thirty mina, since his friends will serve as guarantors. He could have proposed this fine in the first place, but he wanted to outrage the judges, in order to provoke them to kill him.

He is left to make his closing remarks before he is taken to prison to await his execution. He tells the condemners not to be proud for having killed him, as if they have vindicated themselves and taught him a lesson. Had he been shameless and begged, he could have gotten off, but he will not do what is unsuitable for a freeman. Begging would, in truth, have been an insult to them, since it shows no real respect, yet they would rather have this flattery than frankness.

He says to the jurors who have condemned him that while he only dies, they have been convicted by the truth of their wretchedness and injustice. He will be avenged straight away upon his death, and his vengeance will be much harsher to his condemners than their sentence upon him. The jurors who voted to condemn thought that by killing him, they would be released from having to justify their lives, but Socrates was restraining others whose questioning is even harsher than his own. The condemners will have to endure the perpetual doubts of philosophy.

After having turned the table on his condemners, he consoles his supporters with hope. He tells them not to be saddened. His *daimonion* did not oppose his death and, therefore, there is the possibility that at this time his death is good for him. He even argues that his death ought not to be feared: death is either nothingness, or it is a state of migration of the soul. In either case, it is not bad. If it is nothingness then it is like the best sleep one can imagine—a sleep where one does not even dream and that is worthy of the King of Persia himself. And if death is the migration of the soul from one place to another, then it is also a great good, for it means that one will be judged by those who are judges in truth, as well as the demigods who were just in their own lives. And one will associate with the poets Orpheus, Musaeus, Hesiod, and Homer. Socrates can even speak with the ancient heroes who, like himself, were unjustly condemned. In the afterworld he would continue to philosophize, just as he does on earth, and he will even question the heroes just as he questions heroism in Athens. In brief, he will live in the afterlife as he has in this life, the only exception being that there they would not kill him for his questioning, for if the things said are true, they are immortal and would not be mortally wounded by Socratic doubts.

The Socratic myth of the afterlife is a rewriting of the Homeric account of Hades as told by Odysseus. In the Homeric account there is no support for philosophy. Life appears as either tragic or comic, whereas in the Socratic account the life of the philosopher emerges as the life in accord with nature, for only the philosopher can continue with his activity in light of death. The pride and passion of everyone else's life is dissolved by death. Odysseus abandoned his descent into Hades, because death was too terrible to face, whereas Socrates exists even more happily in the afterlife, because he will not face persecution there. The Socratic account of Hades reflects the order of nature. Consequently, the poets are subjected to the same questioning as the heroes and demigods, whereas Odysseus never meets a poet in Hades.

Socrates assures the judges who voted for acquittal that there is nothing bad for a good man, whether living or dead, and that the gods are not without care for men. He provides hope to those who would despair from seeing a good and just man suffer, whereas Homer teaches that there is no cosmic support for justice in the afterlife. The Socratic teaching of the afterlife makes men more reasonable by supporting the life of philosophy and the belief in a just order. Ultimately, Socrates is not even angry with those who condemned him since they cannot harm him. They are only wrong for the error of assuming that they could.

Socrates' final request is to ask of his condemners a favor. He says that if his sons should grow up to care for money, or anything else before virtue, and if they should be reputed to be something when they are really nothing, then the condemners should take on the role of Socrates the gadfly father and pain his sons with piercing questions and doubts. Only then will the jury have treated Socrates and his sons justly. In brief, they should punish with education.

With that last request, Socrates goes away to die and the jury to live, he having lived his life and they living theirs. The final query ending the drama is the question of whose fate is better.

Xenophon's Alternative

Xenophon's *Apology of Socrates* shares with Plato's only the barest of bones. The formal charges and the outcome of the trial are the same, as well as the names of the formal accusers. There is even a superficial similarity with the Platonic Socrates' defense speech. Xenophon's Socrates also refers to his *daimonion* and the Delphic Oracle, but he does so in a manner and context that present to the reader a completely different impression than the one left by the Platonic Socrates. The most striking difference is that Xenophon's Socrates' defense to the jury is only a subplot. The trial is narrated by Xenophon as told to him by a character named Hermogenes. Xenophon says that the others who have written on Socrates' trial touched on his arrogant boasting, but they did not make clear that he had already deliberated and decided that it was best for him to die. Consequently, Socrates' manner of speaking seems imprudent rather than a consequence of reflection and choice about what was best for himself. The other writer in question is of course Plato, and Xenophon's opposition to him provides definition and depth to Xenophon's *Apology*.[73]

---

73 Reeve's introduction to Xenophon's *Apology* captures the differences in character between Xenophon's and Plato's Socrates, but he attributes these differences to Xenophon being a gentleman and not a philosopher. C.D.C. Reeve. *The Trials of Socrates* (Hackett Publishing, 2002), p. 177. Strauss discusses Xenophon's *Apology* and Socrates' act of deliberation in light of Xenophon's other Socratic writings and Socrates' other activities. Leo Strauss. *Xenophon's Socrates* (Cornell University Press, 1972).

Xenophon's *Apology* covers the action of Plato's *Apology*, *Crito*, and *Phaedo* as Xenophon presents Socrates' trial, imprisonment, and death as the continuous action of Socrates' own deliberation. By going behind the scenes and destroying the dramatic illusion created by Plato, Xenophon creates a new Socrates, one of noble and cheerful simplicity. Xenophon's Socrates is clearly both ironic towards and contemptuous of the city. His defense of himself before the jury, in light of his deliberation, has the effect of revealing his irony to the reader. His speech to the jury appears as a mechanism in the greater drama of his own suicide. Serious engagement with the city is totally lacking. Socrates does not appear to die for a higher calling, like a Delphic mission, to know himself and to fulfill his duty as gadfly to the city. His arrogant boasting will not inspire anyone towards a life of questioning that challenges the sacred opinions of the city, never mind the opinions of the sophists and natural scientists. Moreover, Xenophon's Socrates does not tell a myth about Hades or attribute to himself heroic action befitting Achilles. In brief, Xenophon thinks the attempt to turn Socrates into a martyr for philosophy and a master for a cult of ascetics is mistaken. There is nothing dutiful and heroic about Xenophon's Socrates. He has no mission and answers no calling. He lives for the enjoyment of his faculties and for his own self-respect. He is much more self-possessed and less cosmic than the Platonic Socrates, and defends himself more with respect to his moderation than his wisdom. He does not even attempt to discuss his wisdom and relate it to his political duties.

By exposing the dramatic illusion created by Plato, Xenophon also softens the injustice done to Socrates by the city. Xenophon's Socrates invites his guilty verdict. The city appears beneath Socrates' contempt and he shows no desire to be anything to it. He openly insults it and provokes it in order to have it kill him, but such manipulation only proves its stupidity and brutality.

Xenophon does not want to use the tragic passions of terror and pity on behalf of philosophy, whereas Plato encourages guilt and remorse in the entire city for having put to death a semi-divine being, and tells the city a myth about reward and punishment in the afterlife.

The dramatic conflict in Xenophon's *Apology* is less the conflict between philosophy and the city than the conflict between philosophy and a certain kind of man—that man is of course Hermogenes. In Plato's *Apology*, Socrates purposely expands the circle of his accusers so that he can engage the entire city whereas Xenophon consciously limits the audience to a private man. Xenophon's Socrates is less earnest about defending himself to the city than in defending himself against the charges brought by Hermogenes, who admonishes Socrates for not preparing a defense.

Socrates tells Hermogenes that to have gone through life having done nothing unjust is the noblest care for one's defense. Hermogenes is not satisfied with this response because inner confidence in oneself is no protection against the jury who will acquit those who flatter them and condemn those who offend them. The jury is like a god, and its decisions do not reflect justice, but its own sense of itself as a supreme authority. Hermogenes is more impressed by the need to survive such prejudice than he is by Socrates' self-admiration. In other words, Hermogenes approaches the belief that survival rather than self-respect is most important.

In the *Symposium,* Hermogenes explains exactly what it is on which he prides himself. Each speaker must, like a submissive lover, expose himself by confessing what it is that gives him his self-respect. Hermogenes says that he is proud of his friends and the benefits they confer upon him. We learn that his friends are the gods and the benefits they give to him are signs. When he obeys the signs he is rewarded or, at least, not harmed; and when he disobeys the signs he is punished. His pride is his piety, but it is a piety that is directly connected to his own welfare.

Hermogenes practices a kind of bourgeois religion that is devoid of admiration. His religion is the equivalent of what economic indicators are for the modern investor. He fears the world of chance, and from that fear emerge gods who take care of him. His piety is unconnected to reverence for either the gods or himself because his devotion is squarely grounded in his continuous concern for his own well-being. He is said to be one who aspires to gentlemanliness, which is a polite way of saying that he is not a gentleman though he has the capacity to admire them. He is divided between his narrow self-concern and his openness to the possibility that there are things worthy of admiration that are greater than and unrelated to himself.

Socrates says that his death would now be best because his faculties are in decline, and with the decline of his faculties he lives a less pleasant life. With the loss of his faculties he would lose his own good opinion of himself and the confirmation of his superiority from the admiration of others. Socrates presents himself as an aristocratic type whose happiness is drawn mainly from himself, but who also enjoys the confirmation of it. This is in striking contrast to Plato's Socrates who is presented as religious and devoted, and whose mission seems forced upon him.

Consistent with Xenophon's gentlemanly presentation of Socrates is the character of his defense against Meletus. Socrates responds to the accusation that he does not believe in the gods of the city by asserting that Meletus and everyone else has seen him making sacrifices at the altar. The outward deed is supposed to speak for the inward belief because, like a gentleman, he is honest and his actions speak for themselves.

There is no dialogue with Meletus and no attempt to humiliate him by getting him to contradict himself. There is no Platonic refutation. There is certainly no attempt to use the *daimonion* as a refutation against the charge of atheism. Xenophon's Socrates treats the *daimonion* in a less religious manner than does Plato's Socrates. Xenophon's says that the *daimonion* opposed him when he went to give a defense speech, but it did not set him upon a different way of life from the city, as in Plato's *Apology* where the *daimonion* told him to stay out of political life. The *daimonion* is a sound like the sounds made by the oracles and birds. Socrates clearly insults these oracles by calling them "sounds" or "noises", and especially by claiming that his *daimonion* is superior to these other sounds, as is proven by the fact that Socrates never gave out bad advice to his friends. The voice of the divine should be reflected in the human voice, since the divine should reflect the reason of the mind, and not unintelligible mumblings.

Some were jealous of Socrates' voice while others did not believe him. He goes from the frying pan into the fire by recalling the story of the Delphic Oracle to the jury. Xenophon's Socrates says that the oracle declared him most free, just, and moderate, rather than wisest. As high as this praise is, the Oracle did not praise him as highly as he praised Lycurgus, who was compared to a god. Socrates is not a legislator like Lycurgus, or a man who can be followed like a divine authority. Xenophon here clarifies his fundamental disagreement with Plato. Plato, by calling Socrates wise, even if only to attribute to him human wisdom, sets him up as a rival authority to the city. In Xenophon's *Apology*, there is no Delphic riddle and mission. The oracle simply affirms an obvious characteristic recognizable to all—Socrates' moderation.

Socrates reflects on his superior character, but oddly he now speaks of his freedom and wisdom. He is wise because he is most free or least enslaved to his body. By coupling his wisdom with his freedom, and by now mentioning his wisdom instead of his moderation and justice, Xenophon suggests that Socrates' justice and moderation were the effect of his wise indifference to the pleasures of the body and to material goods.

Despite the mention of Socrates' wisdom, it is not thematically discussed and is not part of a divine mission culminating in knowledge of ignorance. To the contrary, Xenophon's Socrates has learned whatever good thing he could. The proof of his wisdom is not his refutation of all other human beings but the fact that others, both foreigners and citizens, associate with him and give to him even though he cannot repay them. He has nothing to offer other than knowledge, and this he calls the delight of the soul, in opposition to the delights of the marketplace and of the body, which consume his fellow citizens. How could Socrates be said to corrupt the young when his wisdom culminates in moderation?

Meletus responds that Socrates persuades sons to obey him rather than their parents. Plato treats this corruption charge as a conflict between Socrates and the laws of the city, whereas Xenophon leaves it at the conflict between Socrates and jealous fathers. As in Plato, Xenophon's Socrates argues that obedience is not always given to relatives but rather to experts. For example, in health, the doctor is obeyed. In assemblies, the most sensible are obeyed, as when the assembly elects as generals those who are most sensible in matters of war. Socrates finds it amazing that he is being prosecuted for a capital offense for being judged by some to be best with regards to the greatest good for human beings—education.

The art of medicine cures the body of disease, and the art of generalship has victory in war as its end, but what is the end of the art of education? Socrates says that education is greater than the knowledge of medicine and of generalship, and thereby suggests that the end of education can be discovered by figuring out how medicine and generalship point beyond themselves to a higher end. Neither medicine nor generalship can be comprehensive because they are ordered by a necessity that they cannot comprehend. Although both disease and violence can cause death, neither is mortality itself. Education would be learning how to die, and Xenophon offers the suicide of Socrates as an example of this education.

Xenophon interrupts the discussion of education to report that, at this point, Socrates' friends spoke on his behalf and that his goal was to appear neither impious as regards gods, nor unjust as regards human beings, and that he also thought it was best for him to die. Like Plato's Socrates, Xenophon's offers no counter-penalty to his death sentence. He says that he will not be humbled by being put to death unjustly, and that shame will belong to those who have condemned him rather than to himself.

The shame, however, that Xenophon's Socrates seeks to instill in the jury is different from the shame elicited by Plato's Socrates. Xenophon's Socrates compares his unjust condemnation to the killing of Palamedes by Odysseus, and states that there is comfort in knowing that Palamedes still occasions nobler songs than Odysseus, who unjustly killed him. Xenophon's Socrates still expects the city and the poets to reign, but he hopes that there will be a small group who remember Socrates and sing his praises. Certainly through the Socratic writings of Xenophon, Socrates will be remembered as a man who "never committed any injustice against anyone, nor ever made anyone worse. On the contrary...gratuitously benefited those conversing with [him], by teaching whatever good was in [his] power"[26]. Xenophon portrays a gentle Socrates, who does not even sting.

Socrates then walked away with beaming eyes and mien and gait. He perceived that those accompanying him were crying and he consoled them by appealing to their reason. He reminded them that from the time he was born he was condemned to death by nature, and that they ought to be cheerful since he is ending his life at a time when good things are flowing in and difficult ones are still on the horizon. Apollodorus, an emotional admirer of Socrates, then said: "Still, Socrates, what is hardest of all to bear, for me anyway, is that I have to watch you being put to death unjustly"[28]. Socrates stroked Apollodorus' head and with a laugh asked him if he would prefer him to die justly or unjustly. Plato tells this Socratic joke in the *Phaedo,* rather than the *Apology,* and the different contexts shed light on Xenophon's intention. Xenophon's *Apology* ends with Socrates' death instead of his unjust condemnation. The effect of this is to soften and even eradicate the sense of injustice done to Socrates by the city.

Socrates then addresses his enemies by way of an omen for Anytus. He says "Now there is a man full of glory, as though he had accomplished something great and noble by killing me, all because when I saw the city considering him as worthy of the greatest offices, I declared that he should not educate his son to be a tanner...I declare, therefore, that he shall not remain in the slavish occupation his father has arranged for him; but since he has not any earnest guardian, he shall fall victim to some shameful desire, and will surely descend further into a base wretchedness"[29,30]. Xenophon vouches for the truth of the prediction. The son of Anytus delighted in wine and did not cease drinking night or day, and finally became worthless to his city, to his friends, and to himself.

In contrast, the Platonic Socrates tells a moral myth about Hades to console the jurors who voted for him and to strike fear into the jurors who condemned him. He warns the condemners that they will not be able to escape the questions of the gadfly by killing him, because his students will carry on where he has left off. Xenophon gives no new myth of Hades and does not speak of the Socratic school continuing through the generations.

Xenophon comments on the end of Socrates' life by saying that he "demonstrated, too, the strength of his soul. For as soon as he discerned that being dead was better for him than to be still alive—just as he was not averse to other good things—he did not weaken in the face of death; on the contrary, he gladly accepted it, and brought it upon himself"[33]. A kind of Stoic cheerfulness characterizes the life of Socrates.

Xenophon ends his narration of the trial of Socrates by saying of his wisdom and nobility that when he reflects upon them, he cannot help but praise Socrates, and that if anyone who aims at virtue were to ever meet a man more helpful than Socrates, that man would be worthy of being thought most blessed. Like a gentle and beneficent god, he compels admiration and gratitude.

Conclusion

Plato's Socrates says that to fear death is to seem to be wise but not to be wise. This statement echoes the *Phaedo* where he says that philosophy is learning how to die. Many men die as heroes and martyrs, and many more commit suicide, but only philosophers die without illusions, which means that only philosophers live without illusions.

Xenophon no less than Plato pointed to this awareness as the distinctive element of the philosophic soul. He differs from Plato in its presentation, and this difference in presentation points to a difference in awareness. Xenophon's Socrates appears to be more frank than Plato's because he openly states that he is committing suicide. He appears as a man of cheerful self-sufficiency and deliberation rather than of divine mission. His nature places him so far above the people that his irony is revealed. He is not a dutiful martyr and is, therefore, less engaged with the city than the Platonic Socrates, who makes claims to the city's highest honors.

Xenophon hides from the audience Socrates' gadfly-like nature. The art of dialectics, so prominent in Plato, is hardly present in Xenophon, whose Socrates presents himself as a man so far from knowing nothing and unable to teach virtue, that he claims to be an educator in the good things, and appears as a wise counselor capable of giving advice to his friends. He is a philosopher-counselor.

In the *Anabasis* 3.1.5, Xenophon asks Socrates for advice about a military expedition. Socrates tells him to consult the Delphic Oracle, which is fitting, since Xenophon wanted to know if the expedition would be successful and if he himself would return home safely. Such a question is for the god and not for a man. Socrates admonishes Xenophon for his question, but no dialogue between Xenophon and Socrates ensues.

Socrates' manly but cheerful acceptance of mortality is more admirable than the nobility of the soldier and even the founder, and gives to the gentleman an example of simple and private grandeur that requires no wealth and no deeds.

Plato, on the other hand, presents a Socrates who is searching and inspired—who is both a dialectician and a diviner of myth. His art of dialectics is at the center of his philosophic nobility. Through it, he confronts the prejudices of the city and carries out his activity. He is possessed rather than self-possessed, and has followers and enemies rather than friends and detractors. He resembles the rhetoricians but is inspired by truth, rather than either money or fame, and because he is characterized by his wisdom, he is in a contest with the highest authorities. He lays claim to deserving the highest honors as well as to being the true poet, for he does not flatter the city but shows it in its true light, which is the light of philosophy.

The different presentations of philosophy are in part caused by different understandings of how to preserve its legacy, and how its example can contribute to having a civilizing effect. Xenophon hopes that a class of gentlemen will find strength and admiration for Socrates, who is neither a tyrant nor a dialectician, but a man of quiet and noble reason. Plato appeals to the cult of reason and transcendence, or to those who are in conflict with the authority of the city and its gods and who seek a higher and purer duty. Xenophon dignifies philosophy in its private capacity, even when it is in the midst of answering public charges, whereas Plato exalts philosophy and allows it to lay claim in public. These differences in presentation are ultimately caused by different understandings of philosophy. Plato is bolder than Xenophon in asserting both the nature and place of philosophy because he thought that man's reason was less self-sufficient than Xenophon thought it was. Reason is connected to the will and needs to make claims on its own behalf.

It may seem contradictory that reason should be in need of claiming its place in the order of being, but this ambiguity is part of its nature. Any attempt to free it from an explanation of its claim, or from its claim itself, is a distortion of its nature. It is coextensive with the will, and the attempt to make it either self-sufficient or to subordinate it to the will distorts its awareness of its own limits and strength. Plato is bolder than Xenophon and more moderate the Nietzsche, and this reflects his awareness of the wisdom of philosophy.

Glossary of Greek Words

Apology (*Apologia*)- An apology is a defense speech. Although it can mean a defense of oneself in court before formal charges, it can also mean a defense of one's life in general. In this sense, an apology is the opposite of an unexamined life.

Gentleman (*Kalos kagathos*)- Literally means noble and good, and has the sense of "gentleman" or one who is neither a hero nor a philosopher, but who lives a life of self-rule and orderly respectability.

Human Being (*Anthrōpos*)- Human being is a term that can be both disparaging and elevating. It can mean an undistinguished member of the many, as distinguished from an *anēr* or manly man. But it can also mean a member of one's species or kind in the highest sense—one who practices the virtue of a human being, as opposed to the virtue of a citizen and of an *anēr*.

Judge (*Dikastēs*)- The root of *dikastēs* is *dikē* (right), which can mean custom, usage or justice. A judge is a jury member and judges in accord with the laws, but Socrates raises the question of who the true judge is, thereby raising the question of what true justice is.

Man (*Anēr*)- A real or manly man. Achilles is the pagan ideal of a real man, but Socrates contests his true independence, and gives the laurel for independence to himself.

Myth (*Mythos*)- Myth is distinguished from logos. Myth is an account that depends upon what is said by others, and especially by tradition, whose authority depends upon the poets and their inspiration.

Philosopher (*Philosophos*)- The philosopher is a lover of wisdom. This meaning is contained in the compounds *philo* (love), and *sophia* (wisdom).

Politician (*Politikos*)- A politician is one who leads in the affairs of the city (*polis*). The city is here understood as being neither cosmopolitan nor political in our sense of the term. The city is not dominated by polite urbanity and entertainments, because it is not insulated from foreign affairs, nor is it impersonal like the state, and constituted by mass devotion like the nation. The city is meant to be beyond the frivolous, the abstract, and the vulgar. It is meant to allow for the full development of human character including the exercise of the faculties. By claiming to surpass the politicians in wisdom, Socrates is claiming a place of greatness and excellence.

Prudence (*Phronēsis*)- *Phronēsis* is a kind of good sense distinguished from *epistēmē* and *sophia*. Xenophon begins his *Apology* by addressing the impression left by Plato that Socrates was, at his trial, *aphrontestera* or without prudence. Xenophon's *Apology* thus appears to provide a bridge between philosophy and men of prudence.

Speech, Reason (*Logos*)- Speech includes certain ideas about what speaking means. Speech can also mean reason or account, and thus implies that speech is connected to a reasoned account or explanation.

Virtue (*Aretē*)- Virtue is the excellence of a thing. Socrates speaks of the virtue of a horse, and even of the virtue of non-natural things such as political offices, judges for instance. The question of virtue is whether or not there is an excellence of a human being. Socrates, the barefoot street philosopher, without money, family, or office, is the test case.

Wisdom (*Sophia*)- Wisdom is the highest kind of awareness and is distinguished from both *epistēmē* and *phronēsis*. *Epistēmē* usually refers to either technical knowledge or to knowledge in general. *Phronēsis* implies prudence or knowledge that leads to decisions and actions. *Sophia* is more closely connected to contemplation, and has as its faculty intelligence (*nous*).